THE SOJOURNER-LADYBUG'S HUMAN

Encountering the Discarded, the Unseen
and the Emotionally Unhealed:
We Need to Become Love

Revised Edition

ISBN Print Edition - 978-1-7772784-2-7
ISBN Kindle Edition – 978-1-777-2784-3-4

Cover design by Ecclesia Publishing
Cover photography by Myriam Greff
www.kintsugi.fr

Any references to historical events, real people, or real places are used by permission or of public domain.

First Printing edition 2019
Revised Edition 2020

Edited, Produced and Published by:
Ecclesia Publishing
Toronto, Canada
www.ecclesiapublishing.com
ecclesiapublishing@gmail.com

Author Contact Information

Ann Bandini can be contacted for any requested information at:

originalrestoredculture@gmail.com

88 N. Avondale Rd. #329 Avondale Estates GA 30003

The Original Restored Culture is our business/training entity

My by-line

"Stopping for the One"

Please visit the Ladybug Loves Project on Instagram

@ Ladybug Loves Project

Podcasts with Ann Bandini on

https://anchor.fm/originalrestoredculture

More training materials and online presence coming soon.

Please check back often.

To be sure you are included in our many projects, send us your email address and request to be added to our online list so you don't miss any of upcoming online training and/or speaking engagements.

Other available books authored by Ann Bandini:

Second Edition Prayer Strategy:

God's Provocative Plan for Wealth

Dedication Of This Book

No matter how you may be perceived or represented here, I want to thank all of you who have been so much a part of this book along the way. I could not have made it without you and the direction and orchestration by G-d, to walk *the sojourner's journey*. The sojourner among you was sent, and you reached out in some way, as it was in your scroll of destiny to embrace the one who was sent to be among you for that season.

I dedicate this book to you and to so many others who supported me in all the ways necessary to bring this book to life. Though I say, *"thank you,"* it feels inadequate, I do pray that this book will become a valued tool for an awakening in your life and in the life of others who will read it. I am flourishing and well today because of your generosity, kindness, love, and obedience.

May this book help in guiding you through difficulties and bring you into a deeper understanding of the release provided for us to shift us from mindsets of bondages and entanglements of the mundane, hence, releasing from the bonds of corruption.

Table of Contents

A Memorial To Ladybug Love

It is with great sadness that I have added to this book, the part that you are about to read. My sweet little fur baby, my precious, delightful, loving Ladybug Love went to Heaven on January 3, 2019.

She had dental work done and went to sleep and went right into the presence of the Lord. How can I express the loss? I have never had the privilege of taking care of something so sweet, loyal and loving, and one who brought so much joy to the world around her.

She was an ambassador of love and joy everywhere she went, and *everybody* loved her. She was tiny, but as soon as she walked into a room, there was joy and there was life. She would put a smile on everyone's face. As you now read our journey, you will want to get involved with her mission, the Ladybug Loves Project. Even as this memorial is written, there is much to prepare in the world around us. Come on in now and follow the life of *The Sojourner—Ladybugs Human.* We invite you on the journey.

~Ann Bandini, the Sojourner

Book Reviews

It is a marvelous wonder to peer into the soul of another person and to empathize with their struggles. It is equally marvelous to feel the rush of emotions when the physical touch of another person relieves them of their suffering. My two favorite sayings are, *"To the world you may be one person, but to one person you may be the world,* and *"I don't care how much you know until I know how much you care."*

Every living being requires love to thrive. Thankfully, many are gifted with compassion and instinctively their radar can pick up on the downtrodden in the blink of an eye. I believe that many can see despair, but if you have lived through despair, you will feel its hopeless desperation.

This account of Ann's journey into a world of struggle without support makes her one of the qualified, whose laser is set to feed the needy. This book shows the burdens a nation inadvertently imposes on its people because most in authority have no clue of how unfair life can be. Sometimes, by our own poor choices and empty pockets we are unable to take care of basic personal needs.

As I read Ann's own experiential journey, I was there with her in heart, and just as Jesus wept, I cried also. People are valuable, and our love should not only be in word but also in deed and this is His call to us all. Our eyes search to and fro looking to stand in the gap to breach the torn and wounded, one life at a time.
~Kathy Allen (Incredible Mother of six adult children and an abundance of grandchildren. This woman is liquid love!)

I was *very* moved by your book! Your sojourner's journey is so important to the Lord — that was oh so obvious to me. I am weeping now as I am so aware that our Lord is "writing" an incredibly beautiful and wonderful story through your life that will bring Him great glory.

The first thing I want to affirm to you is that the Lord has made you uniquely you, and your experiences on this journey are so important to Him. Most of all, I really sensed that throughout the book, you have encountered so many different kinds of people, and you were aware that you were to interact with each of them in a way that is loving to them and healing to you both. This is an expression of the heart of our Father in the distinctive interactions you had with each of them.

I have never been so aware of how each of our lives and our stories are so completely unique. Only our Lord sees and deeply understands each person's life and journey. Your passage on the utter uniqueness of our creation exemplified this so beautifully. You are *very* beautiful, Ann, and our Father sees your beauty most fully and completely, and oh, how He loves you! He fully understands each *'minute'* thing that has formed you and continues to form you. You are revealing HIS glory in and to the whole spiritual world. We on earth, only get glimpses, filtered through our own individual experiences and our knowledge of Him; I see that so clearly through your story. It makes me love HIM and you much more.
~Julie Chambliss (Dedicated to the lives of Refugees)

I would recommend this book because it is the transparent journey of a friend who has walked where many have suddenly discovered their own lives. In it, she reveals her own challenges; and how G-d began to unveil answers, as He revealed His own heart to her. She carries compassion for those who have landed in deep pits through circumstances out of their control. I applaud the hope of a miracle-working G-d that speaks through her pages and shows up as Faithful.
~Laura Harris (Fine Artist)

This book is both timely, and informative! You will be taken on a journey through every page; it's an emotional travel from one place to the next! It is eye-opening, well-spoken and the truth! Great book! You won't want to put it down! One great read!
~Debbie Vaughn (Powerful prophetic voice of our time)

THE SOJOURNER LADYBUG'S HUMAN

Encountering the Discarded, the Unseen,
and the Emotionally Unhealed:
We need to Become Love

The Story

In this book, I have chronicled the many places I've been, my observations and the many people I have met along the way. There are many versions of understanding lifestyles and the family unit, or the environment of the single population, lone parent homes or the downsizing of the growing senior population. The American culture is in deep need today to see things that have shifted radically from previous generations. Just a few short years ago, we have had losses that do not represent what was normal.

This book is a wealth of information and addresses our thinking as our world shifts into a world view that is forever developing in this changing national and international landscape. The United States has been a land known for prosperity, achievement, accomplishment and success but with the freedoms that we have been given, we often can become very impatient, arrogant and ungrateful. Are we abusing these great privileges?

When in comfort, we don't know we have need for change and flexibility, but today's crises call for a provocative change. Comfort must be redefined to see what our ability is to shift our new trending cultural sacrifices.

He executes justice for the fatherless and the widow, and loves the sojourner, giving him food and clothing. Love the sojourner, therefore, for you were sojourners in the land of Egypt. You shall fear the Lord your G-d. You shall serve Him and hold fast to Him, and by His name you shall swear. (Deuteronomy 10:18-20 English Standard Version ESV)

Perspective

I want to take this time to say that in many ways, this book will make you feel a little uncomfortable. It could be the way it is perceived among those who are connected loosely in some way to the circumstances. But the lens that I was given in the fall of 2015 was to see things differently and this has afforded me the ability these past years to live from the "inside looking out" and reporting from this perspective. But the lens that I was given was to *see things differently* in the fall of 2015. I have had the ability, in these years, to live as it is "inside - looking out," and reporting a *perspective.*

I was sent out of my comfort zone to experience this new understanding of who a *"sojourner"* really was, and now I am the reporter who was sent out on a three-year journey. What if every door to all that was comfortable to you was closed, all your things have been disbursed, you're in the middle of moving and you have downsized to the very basic of needs? Though I've never experienced loss from some of the major catastrophic events that have taken place since the beginning of my journey, there have been a considerable amount of very devastating natural disasters across our nation that had huge disruptions and total losses of all possessions instantly! Mudslides, fires, volcanoes, hurricanes and earthquakes. They have had devastating consequences!

Through the events of the last three years, I became aware that now knowingly, I represent so many people who are unseen. Our lives may not have been rattled with a devastation, a displacement, an illness, a divorce or job loss. Or worst yet, "aged out" at 18 years of age with no strong family connections from the foster-care system in America. Unless we experience what it's like to be a sojourner, we will continue to live unaware in our comfortable daily lifestyles.

Today's coming generations are without good role models, proper coaches, mentors or alliances. The latter is known to be riddled with abuses and the unthinkable in the formative years. It is really difficult to attain with the inability to make prudent choices or have the means to do so.

These experiences are foreign to us mainly because we do not walk where they exist. There is a slippery slope for those without compassionate families or a community and networks of caring people to help one from becoming disconnected socially and physically, which is sometimes caused by the lack of identifying papers.

These may be those without a voice in the unseen world who will truly suffer with no spiritual rudder. They have not known how to engage a way to know that G-d will be there for them. Often, man has failed by not understanding that we have been designed to function as a triune being. We are body, mind and spirit called to be part of a tribe. In the current times, this has been very fragmented and non-existent as more and more people are being removed from normal daily life through difficult situations. This will continue until we connect with the reality of a different engagement not found on earth.

As difficult as this journey has been, I always had G-d. Even in my senior years, I have had trepidations, but I also have tenacity and Abba's love for me along the way. I am confident that as I continue maturing in my understanding, He will always be there for me in every situation.

Some may feel parts of this writing are exposing and perhaps, unloving, but we must be realistic about the condition of the human heart until it is healed and restored to its origin. It is G-d's desire to move through us; He wants to shift us attentively in our days on the earth because He has put eternity in our hearts. Remember, as Yeshua began His journey on earth, He stated, *"come and follow me."* We will see that no society can function without the G-d part. We have pushed this to the side far too long, and the connection to Him will continue to be revealed in these matters every day.

"For those whom He foreknew [of whom He was aware and loved beforehand], He also destined from the beginning [foreordaining them] to be molded into the image of His Son [and share inwardly His likeness], that He might become firstborn among many brethren". (Romans 8:29 Amplified Bible, Classic Edition AMPC)

"Then Jesus said to His disciples, If anyone desires to be My disciple, let him deny himself [disregard, lose sight of, and forget himself and his own interests] and take up his cross and follow Me cleave steadfastly to Me, conform wholly to My example in living and, if need be, in dying, also]". (Matthew 16:24 AMPC)

"Keep and guard your heart with all vigilance and above all that you guard, for out of it flow the issues of life". (Proverbs 4:23 AMPC)

The spiritual foundation of so many today is not solid but a walk of depraving difficulty and rebuffing quite akin to the same treatment of the early disciples who suffered much. They were those who walked with Yeshua daily, taking it all in and constantly were reaching out to be the true nature which we are to establish among our fellow man We must be the embodiment of G-d, and often, it is all so very costly. Just to refresh your memory or inform your understanding, this is what Paul the apostle stated:

"Five times I received from [the hands of] the Jews forty [lashes all] but one; Three times I have been beaten with rods; once I was stoned. Three times I have been aboard a shipwrecked at sea; a [whole] night and a day I have spent [adrift] on the deep; Many times on journeys, [exposed to] perils from rivers, perils from bandits, perils from [my own] nation, perils from the Gentiles, perils in the city, perils in the desert places, perils in the sea, perils from those posing as believers [but destitute of Christian knowledge and piety]; In toil and hardship, watching often [through sleepless nights], in hunger and thirst, frequently driven to fasting by want, in cold and exposure and lack of clothing." (2 Corinthians 11:24-27

AMPC)

He expressed that the cost in his leadership role was not one of comfort, but he managed to overcome them all focused on the course. Here, he says, in my natural understanding *"it isn't easy!"* But what if you didn't sign up, you just got elected? What if you said *"yes"*, you stayed in the race and you won't quit? I reiterate, *"Don't quit! Stay in the race!"* As long as you know internally that you are not alone and somehow each day has its own unique sustainability. When G-d allows it, He must guide it! This statement is assigned to you in *"the book that was written for your life"* (according to Psalm 139:16). After all, it's not about me! It's about G-d in me! Though daunting at times, this shows me His omniscience and my inability. This is not always comfortable, but He's the one who has my back and I let Him do it through me!

On this less-traveled road, someone who brought me into their beautiful home wrote me a note from the play, Annie, on a beautiful card, *"The sun will come out tomorrow!"* And the song goes on, *"bet your bottom dollar, tomorrow, tomorrow, is only a day away"* — a discerning heart and affirmations along the path.

THE SOJOURNER LADYBUG'S HUMAN

Encountering the Discarded, the Unseen
and the Emotionally Unhealed:
We Need To Become Love

The Book Cover

The cover I have chosen for this book is a picture of the Kintsugi bowl. In the process of writing this book I came across an article of the Kintsugi bowl, which is the featured on the cover of this book. It was the perfect blend of beauty in art as a piece and representation of the restoration of the human condition to a greater glory.

It spoke volumes to me to know the origin of the Kintsugi bowl. Created out of the fondness for a shattered object, it is the perfect blend of beauty both as a piece of art and as a representation of the restoration of the human condition to a greater glory.

The article is included below for your added enjoyment and also as an explanation of what you may encounter as you journey with me through this book.

It is my desire that it will demonstrate the great need we have today to consider what the Kintsugi bowl represents; broken but beautiful, restored and repaired into a finer, greater glory. It becomes much more valuable as the precious metals used to restore it creates a new, one-of-a-kind piece of art, with veins that make it unlike any other. It becomes priceless because it gives new life to something that has been shattered.

Kintsugi: The Arts Of Precious Scars

Living by author Stefano Carnazzi (Translated from Italian)

By repairing broken ceramics, it's possible to give a new lease of life to pottery that becomes even more refined, thanks to its "scars." The Japanese art of kintsugi teaches that broken objects are not something to hide but to display with pride.

When a bowl, teapot or precious vase falls and breaks into a thousand pieces, we throw them away angrily and regretfully. Yet, there is an alternative, a Japanese practice that highlights and enhances the breaks, thus adding value to the broken object. It's called *kintsugi* (金継ぎ), or *kintsukuroi* (金繕い), literally, golden ("kin") and repair ("tsugi").

This traditional Japanese art uses a precious metal – liquid gold, liquid silver or lacquer dusted with powdered gold – to bring together the pieces of a broken pottery item and at the same time, enhancing the breaks. The technique consists of joining fragments and giving them a new, more refined aspect. Every repaired piece is unique, because of the randomness with which ceramics shatters and the irregular patterns formed that are enhanced with the use of metals. The scars become what to exhibit.

With this technique, it's possible to create a true and always different works of art, each with its own story and beauty, thanks to the unique cracks formed when the object breaks, as if they were wounds that leave different marks on each of us.

The Invention Of The Kintsugi Technique And Its Meaning

The glue traditionally used to bring the pieces together is the *urushi* lacquer, which is being sourced for thousands of years from the *Rhus verniciflua* plant. The Chinese have been using it for thousands of years while in Japan, in the Shimahama Tomb in Fukui Prefecture. Archaeologists found objects including combs and lacquered trays that were used in the Jomon period about 5,000 years ago. Initially, this sticky sap was used for its adhesive qualities to create war and hunting weapons.

The *kintsugi* technique may have been invented around the fifteenth century, when Ashikaga Yoshimasa, the eighth shogun of the Ashikaga shogunate after breaking his favorite cup of tea, sent it to China to get it repaired. Unfortunately, at that time, the objects were repaired with unsightly and impractical metal ligatures. It seemed that the cup was unrepairable, but its owner decided to try to have some Japanese craftsmen repair it. They were surprised at the shogun's steadfastness, so they decided to transform the cup into a jewel by filling its cracks with lacquered resin and powdered gold. The legend seems plausible because the invention of *kintsugi* is set in a very fruitful era for art in Japan. Under Yoshimasa's rule, the city saw the development of the Higashiyama Bunka cultural movement that was heavily influenced by Zen Buddhism, and started the tea ceremony (also called Sado or the Way of Tea) and ikebana (also Kado, way of flowers) traditions, the Noh theatre, the Chinese style of painting with ink.

Even today, it may take up to a month to repair the largest and most refined pieces of ceramics with the *kintsugi* technique, given the different steps and the drying time required. How many beautiful messages do the kintsugi technique conveys?

The Kintsugi Technique Suggests Many Things

We shouldn't throw away broken objects. When an object breaks, it doesn't mean that it is no more useful. Its breakages can become valuable. We should try to repair things because sometimes, in doing so, we obtain more valuable objects. This is the essence of resilience. Each of us should look for a way to cope with traumatic events in a positive way, learn from the negative experiences, take the best from them and convince ourselves that these the experiences make each person unique, and precious.

Who Is A Sojourner?

This term "sojourner or "stranger" refers to a resident alien; a non-citizen in a country where he resides more or less permanently, enjoying certain limited civic rights. This person, the sojourner, is one who actually dwells among other people in contrast to the foreigner, whose stay is temporary.

The term should either be transliterated or consistently be "sojourner" which best agrees with the verb *gûr*. The term was used for the patriarchs in Palate Israelites in Egypt, the Levites dwelling among the Israelites as well as all of the aliens residing among the Israelites.

The sojourner in Israel enjoyed many privileges, a position unparalleled in early legal systems which were usually far from favorable to strangers. Because the sojourner was at a natural disadvantage, he became favored under legislation which was designed to protect the weak and helpless.

Resident aliens (sojourners) are repeatedly mentioned in the historical books; there was a large number in the days of Solomon, apparently, the remnant of conquered tribes. Nationality of such persons followed the father's; according to the son of a *gēr* and a Jewess was a *gēr*.

Legally, the *gēr* had many privileges. The Israelites must not oppress him, in fact; they were to love him. The gleanings of the vineyard and harvest field were to be left for him. He was included in the provision made in the cities of refuge. Although, most legal provisions regard the *gēr* as poor, some apparently, became wealthy. Religiously, nearly all the main holy days applied to the *gēr*:

- He was to rest on the Sabbath.
- To rejoice on Feasts of Weeks and Tabernacles.
- To observe the Day of Atonement.
- To have no leaven on the Festival of Unleavened Bread.
- He was not compelled to keep the Passover but was permitted to do so (if circumcised first).

The Sojourner – Ladybug's Human

So, who is really a Sojourner? And how are we to learn to engage the sojourners whom we will meet along the way? Do you personally know how we are called to treat the sojourners who are learning to navigate the complexities of living in a foreign land? Why have they come into our path, our lives and our community? Let's explore my own life as a sojourner to begin to understand.

I would say on the average, unless one has a Jewish foundation, we do not seek to have an understanding of our obligation or our extension of kindness to build inclusivity in our communities. We really like our status quo and we are not very happy with disruptions.

I found the answers laid out from a biblical perspective about how we can be the temporary extension of love, kindness, and provision on many levels for the needs of the stranger among us.

Do we recognize the sojourners when they come across our busy path or, have we considered how we can build a community to meet their needs? We have been under-educated in this terminology and it is by far an unchartered area. How do we begin to understand how to be available to so many sojourners – it is more than a necessity in the demographic of this changing world.

In many cases, we have the opportunity to be more observant to the things that present themselves to us each day. This can happen if we can pause from our very busy schedules and intentionally look around us. I have learned a lot from being with people in many different environments. G-d specifically identified me as a *"sojourner for a season,"* and I learned much as I inquired from Him about the process that I was to walk through in the early part of my travels. I lived in many different places, situations, homes, Airbnb's, hotels, and even what would be unthinkable — a few stays in my own car.

I had to experience "no place to go" to understand things that can only be experienced from this reality. This happened a few times early on this three-year experience. Few know how to embrace the "stranger among them" for a few nights and I could only trust G-d.

I had to research the reality of a sojourner to understand what G-d was inviting me into. I have learned so much about the Jewish mindset. The Jews that follow the Torah are mandated by a lifestyle that I will share below. They are truly taught that it is their duty to take care of those in need or who are not part of their community. I'm so hungry to learn even more of how this pleases G-d but also trains mankind about our internal obligation to be prepared to help those we encounter and who are the "strangers" among us.

There are many people from the "Christian" persuasion who are coming out from years of the building of institutional churches and becoming what the community needs. This "coming out" shows that often, in current economic flows, forming a blueprint of new ways to assist different cultures and communities are essential to help those who have had losses, devastations or temporary displacement. They are socially, organically and spiritually shifting the nations and becoming connected differently.

Sadly, I don't remember any teachings in the spiritual environments in which I was raised, to be the extension to others in devastation or being available for just "the one." We had no instruction or knowledge about how to encourage us to extend a hand and embrace the people who came into our community. Nothing was established for those who come across our path in this category.

I was not taught how we as a community were obligated to engage and engraft them among us. It didn't come naturally to stop to assist and engage them on their journey in whatever way possible. We are to be part of the provision or a service, a healing or a restoration process in some manner. We are to take the lead and lend a hand. We are to be the needed community. Often, people prefer to be insular.

Introduction

My journey as a sojourner came about at the beginning of 2014 for me. At that time, our nation, the USA, was in a long season of political engineering and unrest. The climate had brought much corruption of our divine Maker's original plan for us as members of the human race.

This situation in my nation was bringing confusion to our most precious commodity—our children and our grandchildren. Much deception was poured out with the intent to shift our culture. The thrust was to indoctrinate a generation with pollution never known since the Second World War and it is on the rise. If continued to go unchecked with no spiritual rudder, we can lose a generation! It has been sinister for us as individuals as a continual seeping of the opposition trying to eradicate our Judeo-Christian foundation and changing our moral compass.

The world stage of the dark underpinnings that many never knew existed was slowly being exposed in bits and pieces. Many began to do their homework. But alas, the world at large has become victims of an age of unprecedented confusion and disruption on a huge social and political scale! In many ways, for the uninformed and the unsuspecting, they are like the proverbial frog placed in a pot of cold water then slowly turning up the heat. For the unsuspecting frog, it is already too late. We can call it *"creeping desensitization."*

A Living Sacrifice Or The American Dream

In 2014, we had so many unbelievable shifts in the American culture, purely through a national political agenda that we could not keep up with, perceive or even take a deep breath. It was a counter-culture agenda to the USA way of life and our belief system, but it was also influencing other nations. Therefore, 2015 was a pivotal year for the USA.

Every single policy was a step further into trampling upon our normal national cultural, values and our sense of what is right, what is wrong, as well as what is actually legal. We have also seen a display which dictates, to superimpose how we think through subliminal language, subtle innuendos and articulations. We have seen the way the leaders who were set into position at that time, speak about us, or the ways they say, *"we believe."* It's blatant social engineering; all lies, and breeds unrest, confusion, and anarchy! It is all subversive and has bred enormous division and confusion.

The national government of the USA was impending on all of our Constitutional rights and privileges, telling us that it is for our greater good to embrace these ideologies. These ideologies are very hedonistic to the core. They are false, with the intention of short circuiting our freedoms. All of this is being done in the deceitful name of "change;" (which was brought to the American people in 2008), under a stupor of political lies and hype—spoken with a swooning language, hence there was a seduction of rational thinking and understanding that the dark man, (not in color but in a seared diabolical agenda) was evil beyond words. He was one who has none of the protocols of having lived in a healthy upbringing that represented the foundational truths, beliefs, and values of how "family life" was to be established. These were not the thoughts of the USA, the American people or how we wanted to live!

There are various compilations of many of the shifts that may not have been voted on by the American people but were pushed out and forced into our "choices." It's alarming to those who desire to keep or restore the integrity of our nation from completely dissolving.

For the uninformed and the novice or the easily dissuaded, the media blitz was slowly corrupting our sacred values of decency, morality, honor, and dignity through our nation and the nations of the world. There was an underpinning of quite a diabolical nature.

Ideologies that we would never tamper with or may have ever been introduced to, we see this entering into the classrooms across our nation, in hopes to stain developing minds with its intent. Without consent, there are things not voted on, being forced on our children to indoctrinate them into things that restricts parental right for consultation. And more than that, there are no voting rights or vetting for these ideologies!

There is something on the peripheral called the reverential fear of the holiness of G-d. Our honorable national byline for years has been IN G-D WE TRUST. He does measure the prayers of those who choose a different position. It is an engagement that we can embrace to offset the evil reports. Heaven's frequencies are available for anyone who needs the impossible. We need a new blueprint to shift our culture. Everything is changing; nothing is business as usual. Engaging truth comes from a *strong spiritual foundation*.

In the west, this is not politically correct but in the south, people understand that G-d is the true source of everything we are. We are shifting ideologies, and no man can stand alone forever without a true G-d connection. It is going to be impossible to try to live a G-dless life pushing an anti-G-d agenda, for every casual way that it is being packaged will disappear.

When faced with where I was in September of 2015, I simply said, *"G-d, what's the plan?"* He responded with, *"you're going to be a sojourner for a season, you're going to see things through a different lens, and you're going to become the message."* I knew it truly would be orchestrated by Him and given that I am senior in age, a very different assignment. I would be in the humblest of normal situations with insurmountable obstacles, needs, and perspective. It would shake a lot of foundations of perceived comfort and would allow me to see the deepest needs of humanity around me from a straightforward position.

The Sojourner Ladybugs Human has been written from my long journey encountering people along the path with little Ladybug, a very sweet 5lb toy poodle, as my constant companion. Her story of loneliness, and the need for deep nurturing gave way to how I have perceived the nature of people along the journey. I have been allowed to walk as one who had no permanent home for three years. This is a true sojourner or known in the Hebrew language as *Ger*.

Ladybug Love: A 5-lb Toy Poodle

I was yet to meet Ladybug, but her life could not have been more in need of change as mine. She came into my life in the second month of my travels and became my own in the fourth month. I wrote her story immediately.

I was taken out of comfort and thrust into a whole new world. I would be meeting people whom I would never have engaged had I stayed in my comfortable 55+ building in Orange County, California. I have been in a total of five states encountering many things and literally meeting people from all parts of the world. And yes, the hand of G-d has allowed each step!

I have also added a lot of information and statistics that the novice may not take the time to research. We can see the path forged in our nation, and the nations of the earth. If we look only to the ensuing cultural shifts and don't become circumspect to identify how to participate in the constantly changing landscape, we will miss our personal opportunity to be used in unusual ways. Be prepared to become part of the solution as we all have a part to play.

My heart's desire is for you to be engaged, changed and to be compelled to come out of any comfort or complacency and to do your part today in a very intentional way, to serve those in your sphere of influence. We can no longer remain insular when the world at large needs community for the plight our nations have become. We need to become the message or answer to those we meet along the way and build a protection for the vulnerable and the disenfranchised.

This Is My Story And My Journey

The Cities Of Irvine-Tustin, California

I lived for seventeen years in Irvine, California, which has been known annually, as number one for the top ten safest cities in America. Comparatively, Irvine is America's safest city because of its size, according to the latest FBI statistics. In 2019, the FBI's Annual Uniform Crime Report also showed that Irvine had the lowest rate of Part 1 violent crime for cities of 250,000 people or more. That included murder, rape, robbery, aggravated assault, burglary, larceny-theft, auto-theft, and arson.

That marked the 12th consecutive year that Irvine has earned the Safest City designation. During the time I lived there, no major crimes of great consequence was ever recorded. At least, there was nothing that challenged the gentle landscape of comfortable peaceful central and south Orange County.

In 2011, I simply needed lower housing costs and began my research. I was fortunate to be directed to a brand-new 55+ senior building that was taking applications and in the process of being built. I was going to be able to decrease my monthly payment by $500.00 a month, truly a prudent move in an expensive housing market.

I moved to Tustin in 2012, within four miles of my residence to an equally beautiful community right on the Irvine border built on a sprawling former military base which was now closed. It was right behind the huge contemporary shopping center called The District, which opened in 2008.

Now that I live outside of California, I can see the prices of housing and rentals in this geographical area are still in an unaffordable range.

Housing and related living expenses in Orange County alone, have increased and soared by the alarming amount of $5,000.00 per household in the year 2017 alone. Based on what the rest of the country's housing costs are, California has some of the most expensive, rapidly growing real estate and rentals in our nation.

Rents and sales are much lower in states outside of California and are still on the low end of what rents were seven years ago in Orange County, California. which has now accelerated, out of control. However, in the few years I've been living away from California, the housing problem has increased drastically in that state as well as around our entire nation. There is now a disproportionate challenge among middle and lower-class people. The simplicity of a casual life has been dulled by the ever-growing loss of affordable housing in a state that once drew people from all around the country.

Losing Your Home

Scott Baxter, 57, an Orange native, stacked his neatly packed possessions at the front of his tent, south of Orangewood Avenue. He said he'd already stashed the rest of his belongings – clothes, blankets and canned goods – in a concealed locale in the city of Orange, where he said he planned to begin living in a couple of days. *"I know I've got to go,"* said Baxter, who said that he lost his job in 2014 as a union plumber, when he was injured after the home he was living in, exploded. *"The deputies tell us, 'If we see you making an effort, that's all we need.'"*

Here is a gentleman who was moved to the streets by extreme adversity with no place to go. It is a travesty. He was ousted from a homeless encampment that formed along the Santa Ana riverbed in Anaheim, California very near to Disneyland, which is called "the happiest place in the world." This was documented in 2018.

This is so painful to read. It hurts, as can be seen in a recent statement made on Facebook by Christina Shea, a resident, who is a long-term politician in Irvine. She is the one who fought for the city of Irvine in its local government for years. She is the one who has brought much good to the dynamics of some of the political dilemmas facing this pristine city.

Here is what Christina posted on her Facebook page: *"Today, Federal Judge Carter will meet with city reps to discuss a County wide solution to our homeless problem. Irvine has been way ahead of the curve helping our lower income, our veterans, our single moms and dads and our homeless population. Tonight, at City Hall at 7:00 pm, we will have an update from our Mayor, and hopefully, Supervisor Spitzer, to hear what was discussed in the courtroom this morning. I will see you there!"*

Now here is the cold, uneducated, hardened response in great ignorance from one of the local readers and I quote: Natalie Golovin says: *"It will just get worse. 'Homeless' is a nice word for what used to be called 'bums.'"* G-d have mercy on our challenges and open up our compassion and humility, to form alliances with those who are moving forward to be the solution to this huge growing national problem throughout our land!

A Deep Conflict Of Our National And Cultural Shift.
(Though we never voted on it or agreed with it)

In 2013 I was in the planning stages to host one more event in Orange County. I knew I would be leaving the area soon and wanted to the complete the assignment, however, there was so much conflict with the planning, I was at a loss. In hindsight, I can see why we could not get it done. Each time there is a cultural shift and transition that starts on earth, there has been a spiritual opposition, and conflicting war waged from the heavens to earth. We need to know the unseen realm.

Here is a view from scripture to express the experience of Daniel, who was shifted into the political climate that he endured, as he held his position in his day. He and his three companions, who are also Hebrews, had been sent and thrust as servants into a whole new culture, completely, politically and spiritually opposite to theirs. Here is some of their story.

Daniel chose to live a fasted lifestyle which also empowered his discernment. He entered into a heavenly realm contending Heaven to earth. He went past barriers of spiritual climate, calamity, and opposition. Reading from Daniel 1:1 -

"And the [Babylonian] king told Ashpenaz, the master of his eunuchs, to bring in some of the children of Israel, both of the royal family and of the nobility—Youths without blemish, well-favored in appearance and skillful in all wisdom, discernment, and understanding, apt in learning knowledge, competent to stand and serve in the king's palace—and to teach them the literature and language of the Chaldeans."

They were from the very best and the top of the line in Hebrew culture. They carried a spirit of discipline and excellence and were thrown into a completely new and foreign culture. When you step into a political arena that is a hotbed of compromise, debate, and lacking ethical foundations, people need to do more than make a political statement. Often, they *are* the statement and the message. This is played out in the story below of Daniel from the Bible and the unseen realm.

Daniel had fasted for twenty-one days because of the political climate on earth. As he continued to pray, he entered "behind the veil," spiritually because of his close connection to the Hebrew G-d. In that realm, he supernaturally encountered the most magnificent of angels, Michael; the *chief* of the celestial angels, and here is what his prayers produced. Daniel was not a lightweight to opposition, and he knew the cost to maintain his integrity and ground. He also knew the possible consequences.

It is a sobering thought to know the mettle of the man who would not bow to the gods of this world. He continued to follow the path forged for him in the affliction and politics of his day. Wow, what an example and role model especially for the next generation today! No compromise!

"In the third year of Cyrus king of Persia a message was revealed to

Daniel ... and the message was true, and it referred to great conflict (warfare, misery). And he understood the message and had an understanding of the vision. And I, Daniel, alone saw the vision [of this heavenly being], for the men who were with me did not see the vision; nevertheless, a great panic overwhelmed them, so they ran away to hide themselves. So, I was left alone and saw this great vision; yet no strength was left in me, for my normal appearance turned to a deathly pale, and I grew weak and faint [with fright]. Then I heard the sound of His Words; and when I heard the sound of His Words, I fell on my face in a deep sleep, with my face toward the ground." (Daniel 10:1a, 8 AMP)

Fear Not...Daniel Comforted

"Then behold, a hand touched me and set me unsteadily on my hands and knees. So, He said to me, "O Daniel, you highly regarded and greatly beloved man, understand the words that I am about to say to you and stand upright, for I have now been sent to you." And while He was saying this word to me, I stood up trembling. Then He said to me, "Do not be afraid, Daniel, for from the first day that you set your heart on understanding this and on humbling yourself before your G-d, your words were heard, and I have come in response to your words. But the prince of the kingdom of Persia was standing in opposition to me for twenty-one days. Then, behold, Michael, one of the chiefs [of the celestial] princes, came to help me, for I had been left there with the kings of Persia. Now I have come to make you understand what will happen to your people in the latter days, for the vision is in regard to the days yet to come." When He had spoken to me according to these words, I turned my face toward the ground and was speechless." (Daniel 1:10)

I felt the great need to lay this political information out to the community I lived in, so I planned a conference type event. Through doing so, we can form a position of strength with one's deep spiritual foundation. It displays an understanding of the heart, by bringing needed information to produce this type of planned event. This would have more political overtones than the other conferences that I had hosted in the past with selected leaders. One proposed guest would eventually be a candidate, who would later run for the office of the president of the USA in our next election.

The other speaker, who had spent twenty years travelling the USA as a TV producer, was given a very significant spiritual assignment. He was deeply connected to G-d. As a businessman he would be sent throughout our nation in a position of humility, repenting for the deep iniquity in our land. He had attended the first business training event that I had been commissioned to host in 2001 in Southern, California. He has produced many small feature documentaries on the powerful, historical, political, spiritual revelations and encounters he had experienced in our nation and other nations, in video form. These are very enlightening and educational of many foundational truths in our nation.

I was excited to reunite with him, as I shared a message from 2002 that I spoke in Atlanta, Georgia. It was called, *"when the World Trade was hit on 911, World Economics Went into Chaos and Will Never Recover."* I concurred with much of what he had gotten on the shifts in our nation. But unknown to me, he had many more years of experience with a multitude of heavenly encounters that G-d had ordained, which far surpassed my understanding. People needed to hear these things in Orange County.

Because of scheduling dates for these two important leaders, plus the designated location of the conference, which was the only location available, the event could not be accommodated so it all fell through. I decided to just release it and move on. It became overwhelming but left me knowing I had to delve further than ever to understand what all of us needed to know about our world in chaos.

2014 - A Year Of Research, Study, And Fasting

The next step was to get understanding. It had to be drastic and focused. This year was different, as our nation was in chaos and crises. World governments clashed and ours was in a fog of undiscovered and matchless deception along with a dark, sinister undertow that was like no other time in modern history.

Things were not right, and we knew it, but the exposure was not as visible as we needed to know. We would have to wait two more years before the veil would be cleared as the darkest of the dark as sinister corruption would begin to unravel in every sacred venue. One could not imagine how major moral values had given way to the likes of gangsters in years gone by. The provocation of the hidden immorality, corruption, perversion and much more was only exposed to those who would take the time to do the research *and those who engaged in prayer.*

A major part of our moral fabric was being torn down, one shred at a time. Our values were being socially engineered, and we were in the slumber of catastrophic proportion. Our next generation was now in its sixth year of militant left-wing education, distortion and political agenda like no other. They believed what their instructors said as undeniable truth and without personal discovery, *"drank the Kool-Aid"* offered at the fountain of immeasurable hedonism, which our nation has never known. Without a spiritual rudder, radicalization was taking place at an unprecedented pace.

We were told by the extreme left-wing that our beliefs were through fake media and social engineering. They thought they could shape a moral choice and destroy the structure upon which our honorable, sacred nation was developed. We have always been a place of freedom from tyranny and have valued human dignity. But alas, things have gone radically wrong, and the strength of *"In G-d We Trust,"* had all been wiped off in an attempt to dismantle our entire nation. It has been beyond horror as we see what we know is morally right but has been packaged as politically incorrect. Our judicial system has crumbled by some who uphold laws of intimidation and support the debased in our sociality. The fight has been fierce.

The last few years of my season of travels, have been to experience those who have been displaced and have been forced to a much lower standard of living. In recent generations, we have never seen a great corruption and divide in the USA as seen in the twenty-first century.

The Difficulties Of The State Of California

Whether it's California's warm climate or mild winters—it's beautiful coastal drive on Highway one was spectacular for enjoying its beauty. So many vacationers are delighted with the charm of the Bay Area, the Golden Gate Bridge, and the huge Redwood forests in the north in Marin County, Napa Valley's wine country. It's recreational playgrounds like San Diego, the ever-crowded Disneyland and other Southern California amusement parks are great for family fun. California is also home to the entertainment capital of the world, Hollywood, and all the trappings that go with it. Yes, California draws many, but now the mass exodus out of California is formidable and massive. It is plagued with political problems, and the people are groaning.

In 2017, massive fires engulfed the entire state in some very elite locations and from the side of prosperity, now even the wealthy were "homeless" or at least, tragically displaced from the trappings of luxury with fires, floods, and mudslides. This situation spanned from the north in the exotic wine country of Napa Valley to the luxury of Montecito in Santa Barbara County, a place of great wealth and homes of well known, well celebrated people.

Here Is A Most Recent Report From Santa Barbara County, California

Hundreds of people are sleeping in parking lots in areas like Santa Barbara. The rising cost of rent and housing has forced middle class workers to take up residence in their cars to make ends meet. Most of those sleeping "rough" in cars are part of the area's Safe Parking Program, run by the New Beginnings Counseling Center and aims to provide a secure area for the homeless to sleep in their vehicles.

Half The State's Households Struggle To Afford The Roof Over Their Heads.

Homeownership, once a staple of the California dream, is at its lowest rate since World War II. Nearly 70 percent of poor Californians see the majority of their paychecks go immediately to escalating rents. Median earnings for Californians are higher than the national average and are significantly higher in certain regions like the Bay Area and Silicon Valley with tremendously pricey costs of living. But on the average, income over the past two decades has not kept pace with escalating rents. The problem here is not just housing. Income inequality and wage stagnation in California also hinder low and moderate-income households' ability to pay for a home.

The New Normal - Orange County's Escalating Cost Of Living

A family of four with an annual income of $84,450.00 or less now qualifies as low income in Orange County, California. In 2018, a single person living alone qualifies as low income if he or she earns $58,450.00 or less a year. Orange County has the fifth highest income threshold in the nation, according to new income limits released last month by the U.S. Department of Housing and Urban Development.

Government and private agencies use HUD's (Housing and Urban Development) income calculations to determine eligibility for a wide variety of assistance programs, ranging from rent subsidy vouchers and public housing to mortgage assistance. While low-income families qualify for some programs, others are limited to household earnings of far less, with limits as low as $31,300.00 for a family of four.

Record-high rents and home prices are driving up Southern California income limits. Orange County apartment rents, for example, increased by twenty percent over the past seven years (at the time of this book's first edition), while the median sale price of an Orange County house has jumped by forty percent.

"When you tell somebody that's making $70,000 that they're low income, they go, 'What? That's low income?' Unfortunately, that's what comes from living in a high-cost county," said Cesar Covarrubias, executive director of the Kennedy Commission, an Irvine-based affordable housing advocacy group. *"That makes it difficult for working families at all levels."*

Under the 2017 figures, Orange County's income threshold for a family of four jumped by $5,450.00 from the previous year 2016 level. The only metro areas with higher income limits are San Francisco; Fairfield County, Connecticut; Silicon Valley and Honolulu. Even a six-figure salary doesn't *"cut the mustard"* in San Francisco, Marin, and San Mateo counties. A family of four there earning $105,350.00 or less now is considered low income according to HUD figures. Orange County income limits for a family of four exceed Philadelphia's ($66,550.00), Seattle's ($72,000.00), Los Angeles County's ($72,100.00), San Diego's ($72,750.00) and Boston's ($78,150.00).

What Is Happening To Our American Culture?

What has been the symbol of America? Apple pie, Mom, patriotism, honor, respect, and kindness to our fellow man and being neighborly. Where is this now? Have we become so desensitized that we don't really stop along the way to find out how best we can engage those in our geographical areas?

Because of the descent of re-engineered, hidden and unchecked radicalization, there has been a bending of our nation's set of rules and regulations. Leaders are using our constitutional freedoms against its original intention and we are in a mess because militants from the Muslim nations are brought to our very shores. We are a Judeo-Christian nation, and all who come here are to be transitioned into the Republic of our nation. We are a Republic, not a Democracy. The challenge is understanding our beginning and honoring it. It should be made mandatory for everyone in our nation to have Civic Studies refreshed because our education system has failed to keep the truths of our foundation, our constitution and history relevant to the younger generations. The altering of our very competitive education system has completely left the honor and support to this out.

The deep indoctrination of false perceptions such as Marxism and communism have been the cause of the unrest opposing the freedoms of the nation. There have been deceptive factions of race baiting, dividing of people groups, lacking a moral consciousness and respect for human dignity and life in general. One of our symbols of freedom is the Statue of Liberty. And truly, liberty is a spiritual symbol which we must retain for our freedoms today.

The verse most closely associated with the statue, *"Give me your tired, your poor, your huddled masses yearning to breathe free ..."* these words were not added to the pedestal until 1903 after officials realized what an inspiration the statue had become to the waves of immigrants arriving at nearby Ellis Island. The verses are part of The New Colossus, a sonnet composed by New York poet Emma Lazarus in 1883; she donated it to an auction at the New York's Academy of Design to raise money for the statue's pedestal.

This is just one symbol of how we have engaged a sense of *true freedom* that our country has previously been known for and were at rest in.

According to the Merriam-Webster Dictionary, the meaning of *liberty* is; *the quality or state of being free*:

- The power to do as one pleases.
- Freedom from physical restraint.
- Freedom from arbitrary or despotic control.
- The positive enjoyment of various social, political, or economic rights and privileges.
- The power of choice.
- A right or immunity enjoyed by prescription or by grant: privilege.
- Permission, especially to go freely within specified limits was given the liberty of the house.

Can A Nation Be Saved In A Day?

Let's read this!

"Who has heard of such a thing? Who has seen such things? Shall a land be born in one day? Or shall a nation be brought forth in a moment? For as soon as Zion was in labor, she brought forth her children." (Isaiah 66:8 AMPC)

Never in the history of the world had such a thing happened before, but G-d keeps His word. As definitely foretold here and in (Ezekiel 37:21-22 AMPC)

"Then say to them, thus says the Lord G-d: Behold, I will take the children of Israel from among the nations to which they have gone and will gather them from every side and bring them into their own land. And I will make them one nation in the land, upon the mountains of Israel, and one King shall be King over them all; and they shall be no longer two nations, neither be divided into two kingdoms anymore."

Israel became a recognized nation, actually *"born in one day."* After being away from their homeland for almost 2,000 years, the Jews were given a national homeland in Palestine by the Balfour Declaration in November 1917.

The Challenging Precursor; The Eroding Of Character And Moral Fiber In Our Nation In The Mid '90s -
The Shifts In The '90s.

We prayed for corporate America in the '90s; that was my primary assignment. There was a surge to leave the institutions of religious buildings and provide a form of "new awakening" in the marketplace.

In the first book that I was commissioned to write, I addressed the need for balance and also the need for a proper spiritual foundation to offset the heady wealth and prosperity which is so prevalent in the area I lived, specifically, in my home territory, Southern California.

I would take daily walks for an hour and a half for years along the bike path near my residence in Irvine. This was always a very deep time of prayer. I would extend my hands to the corporate buildings and often, in those days, I would weep. Little did I know what was ahead for our nation or the world stage for that matter!

I had already studied the disturbing plight and the corruption as well as the dismantling of our nation's corporations in the '90's through the Enron and Country Wide real-estate mortgages. Justice was served by the imprisoning of the guilty, but people suffered devastating financial losses. The scriptural truth that *"the love of money is the root of all evil"* is evidenced in the corruption of wealth which is obviously influenced and manipulated by the spirit of mammon.

The investing public have been made aware of the fraud and misrepresentation in the presentation of Enron's financial statements, in which the accounting firm of Arthur Andersen appears to have been complicit. At least, 143 corporate clients, out of 2,311, have left Andersen, and Andersen itself has been forced to lay off about 7,000 of its 26,000 employees. All of these failed leaders of Enron Corporation Crises, Arthur Anderson Accounting firm, and Country Wide real estate mortgages, went to jail, and people suffered devastating financial losses.

Bernie Madoff - The Sins Of The Father

And the ultimate heist of that century would come upon us, the appearance of the invincible Bernie Madoff, whose father, unfortunately, was a corrupt businessman as well! The iniquity was generational and passed onto Bernie in his future business dealings.

"You shall not bow down to them or serve them, for I the Lord your G-d am a jealous G-d, visiting the iniquity of the fathers on the children to the third and the fourth generation of those who hate Me." (Exodus 20:5)

"The Lord passed before him and proclaimed, "The Lord, the Lord, a G-d merciful and gracious, slow to anger, and abounding in steadfast love and faithfulness, keeping steadfast love for thousands, forgiving iniquity and transgression and sin, but who will by no means clear the guilty, visiting the iniquity of the fathers on the children and the children's children, to the third and the fourth generation." (Exodus 34:6-7)

If there was ever a case for understanding the deeply entrenched generational bloodline or seed line of iniquity and corruption from one generation to the next, this story resonates. This one leaves a deep, unchecked heavy scar over our nation, and how we moan!

Records of Bernard Lawrence Madoff's (father of Bernie Madoff), financial dealings show they were less than successful with the trade. His mother registered as a broker dealer in the 1960s, listing the Madoffs' home address in Queens as the office for a company called Gibraltar Securities. The Securities and Exchange Commission (SEC) forced the closure of the business for failing to report their financial condition. The couple's house also had more than $13,000.00 in tax lien which went unpaid from 1956 until 1965. Many suggested that the company and the loans were all a front for Ralph's backhand dealings to which Bernie Madoff reportedly admitted to investigators on March 12, 2009, that he had lost $50 billions of his investors' money, and pled guilty to eleven counts of felony, securities fraud, investment adviser fraud, mail fraud, wire fraud, three counts of money laundering, false statements, perjury, false filings with the United States Securities and Exchange Commission (SEC), and theft from an employee benefit plan.

While the extent of his fraud is still being uncovered, prosecutors said $170 billion had been moved through the principal Madoff account over decades, and that before his arrest, the firm's statements showed a total of $65 billion in accounts. Madoff was imprisoned until a sentencing hearing scheduled for June 16, 2009. He was sentenced to 150 years in prison on June 29, 2009—the maximum possible prison sentence for the 71-year-old defendant.

His Sons Mark Madoff And Andrew Madoff

On the second anniversary of his father's arrest, Mark Madoff woke up at 4 a.m. in his apartment in New York City and emailed his lawyer, asking him to take care of his family. He also texted his wife, Stephanie, who was on vacation with their daughter at Disney World, to tell her he loved her and to suggest she send someone to care for their son Nick. Nick, just 22 months old, slept soundly in his bedroom while his father looped a vacuum cleaner cord around a pipe in their living room and tried to hang himself. The cord snapped, so he tried again with the leash of their family dog, Grouper. He was dead by the time his father-in-law arrived, urged by a frantic Stephanie to rush to their home as soon as possible when she got her husband's text.

Mark Madoff was an innocent victim of his father's monstrous crime. *"Mark Madoff took his own life today,"* Mark's lawyer, Martin Flumenbaum said in a statement to the press on December 10, 2010. *"He was an innocent victim of his father's monstrous crime who succumbed to two years of unrelenting pressure from false accusations and innuendos."* Madoff's son, Andrew died of cancer with a $16 million estate he shared with his estranged wife. His girlfriend's court papers had this information. Papers filed in Manhattan Surrogate's Court showed Andrew Madoff owned an estimated $11 million in "personal property" and $4.5 million in real estate when he died of blood cancer. In his will, which was made public on that Thursday, the master scammer's scion left one-third of his property to his wife, Deborah West, and $50,000.00 a month to the woman he described as his fiancée, Catherine Hooper. *"I request my executor to pay to Catherine Hooper, so long as she is living, the sum of $50,000.00 on the first day of each month, commencing thirty days after the admission of this will to probate, for her support until the administration of my estate is completed,"* says the will, which was dated July 8 of that year.

After the estate was completed, she was to be paid from a trust which will have an undisclosed sum of money in it. His two children, who were left all of their father's personal property were also receiving trusts.

Bernie, His Wife; His Childhood Sweetheart, Ruth Madoff

Ruth Alpern met Bernie Madoff when she was sixteen, and they were attending Far Rockaway High School in Queens. Both she and Bernie grew up in a middle-class Jewish neighborhood in Laurelton. They married in November 1959 when she was eighteen.

The Jewish Ketubah: What Every Marriage Should Have

In the Jewish faith, there are five steps to engagement called the Ketubah. It begins with a commitment and a courtship. It is really a spiritual "marriage contract". It is a beautiful document that has these five stages to engage in seeking a young woman with the intent to marry. This document is sacred; it is written out by the couple to be married, negotiating the desires and intent of their union. It is written on a very ornate scroll and signed at the wedding, as part of the sobriety and commitment to the sacredness of holy matrimony. I feel this is one of the most beautiful passages of truly knowing the commitment and honor of covering a wife and being the proper husband and leader of the family.

These five steps are Lecha, Segula, Mikvah, Ketuba, Chuppa. This is so missing in today's society, as marriage is now planned without a long-term understanding of the power of commitment and the union of divine expression. The fortitude for weathering long enduring relationships will now be taught this important factor to success. We need a reset button for the next generation as we launch much needed teachings in the days ahead. The power of negotiating a commitment of honor and knowing one's responsibility to provide and protect a "bride" is essential. This will be the wholesome foundation to raising a solid family, with values to teach the most basic of successes to your treasured children.

If this union had prepared the Madoffs for their Jewish wedding Ketubah as the foundation of their home, it was a true violation of severing the commitment and vows intended to protect the family unit; another part of this tragic twenty-first century corruption on the very fabric of the Madoffs Jewish culture.

Ruth worked as a bookkeeper for Bernie in the investment business he started in 1960. They had been married for sixty years but she maintained that she didn't know her husband was running a Ponzi scheme. After staying with her sister in Florida for several years, Ruth now lives alone in Old Greenwich, CT, in a 989-square-foot condominium. She is still a desirable mark for the paparazzi who have captured her at Ikea and CVS, chic as ever at age seventy-six, in white button-downs and loafers. She still drives a Prius, and she carries an old Goyard handbag, living off the $2.5 million that federal prosecutors granted her in exchange for forfeiting every single other asset (including old clothes and memorabilia; anything that could possibly be sold at auction). She must report any purchase she makes that's over $100.00 to a bankruptcy trustee.

Weep in despair for this brokenness from where G-d resides in Heaven and learn to legislate His magnificent love over the brokenness of leadership on the earth! Those who should have touched lives in an exemplary way with huge transformation are now tethered to the torment of false prosperity and mammon. What have touched lives in an exemplary way with huge transformation are now tethered to the torment of false prosperity and mammon. What have we become? Calloused, materialistic, uncaring, dividing, and tearing asunder instead of engaging our birthright and building up structures of protection and multiplication for future generations. From the most heartless of all, we can derive the loss of what should be our original intent. In seeing all of this, there are scriptures that come to mind as quoted below,

"For men will be lovers of themselves, lovers of money, boasters, proud, blasphemers, disobedient to parents, unthankful, unholy, unloving, unforgiving, slanderers, without self-control, brutal, despisers of good, traitors, headstrong, haughty, lovers of pleasure rather than lovers of G-d, having a form of G-dliness but denying its power. And from such people turn away!" (2 Timothy 3:2)

"But as the days of Noah were, so shall also the coming of the Son of man be. For as in the days that were before the flood they were eating and drinking, marrying and giving in marriage, until the day that Noah entered into the ark, And knew not until the flood came, and took them all away; so shall also the coming of the Son of man be." (Matthew 24:37-45 KJV)

I do believe that there are two camps arising—good and evil—but the confusion is incalculable. It is a sacrificial cost along with the business community crises stated below. Biblically, we must understand from the book of Genesis, which is the very pivotal message of the fruit of the tree of knowledge of good and evil!

The Deceptive Housing Bubble Of 2008: The Mortgage Crises

Much difficulty arose in 2008 with the housing bubble crises, the fall and imploding of a false economy as people lost momentum, real estate, jobs, positions, lifestyle, and hopes to live the lives that they previously held as comfortable. Sources say that that co-founder of the mortgage lender Countrywide, Angelo R. Mozilo, in talks to settle SEC charges, is accused of civil fraud and insider trading.

Kenneth L. Lay, whose father was a "Christian" leader, catapulted Enron Corp. into the ranks of the nation's largest companies, only to be convicted of fraud after its collapse, died early yesterday (July 5, 2006), after suffering what a family spokeswoman said, *"was a heart attack at a rental property in Old Snowmass, Colorado."*

"But You, O G-d, will bring down the wicked into the pit of destruction; men of blood and treachery shall not live out half their days. But I will trust in, lean on, and confidently rely on You".
(Psalm 55:23 AMPC)

"The reverent and worshipful fear of the Lord is the beginning (the chief and choice part) of Wisdom, and the knowledge of the Holy One is insight and understanding". (Proverbs 9:10 AMPC)

Middle-Class Americans, have for the most part, been living in comfort, but that has really shifted over the last decade. We have seen with our own eyes, the eroding ability to sustain the high standard and the American dream. Many people and businesses have left the state of California to settle in places that are more in tune with the changing landscape.

Texas alone has bragged about receiving 1000 people per day, who are moving into its great state in 2016. This is happening because of the wholesome values, a business-friendly environment and a sound political stance of *pro USA*. The freedoms that we hold dear are more valued here in this one state that is self- sustaining in so many ways and completely debt free.

The beauty of Texas is the spacious amounts of land, the friendliness of the people; the state's transportation corridor has been revamped and is in magnificent order. Construction is booming and housing is affordable. My only personal challenge or rant about Texas was the extreme summer heat and a lot of dirt floors for eating areas.

Resilience and a loving heart are the most needed layering over the human condition. And though this paints a good picture, there are issues that have cause us to shifted away from this. But there is also a realm of G-d's supernatural path of goodness, gentleness, meekness, and joy that is available to tap into daily. Engaging in this supernatural pathway has the ability to shift the frequencies and culture of what is trying to unhinge these indomitable values via those who want to see these changes. These changes begin with an individual!

Preparations To Leave California: September 12-15, 2015

My daughter relocated to Austin, Texas in 2013. She worked in the tech business and had a lot of challenges living in the bay area, where my brother's family lived. It was difficult to find local employment providing her with a feasible benefits package and from where she could commute without hours on the road. It finally came to a climax when she had to leave a job which had a four-hour round-trip commute. I suggested Austin, Texas, a booming tech area, for her next choice.

Young people in the bay area were living communally in dorm type buildings for $2,000.00 a month or paying the likes of $5,000.00 for just a one-bedroom place to live in mid-market tech district of downtown San Francisco. It was insane like this in 2013 but has escalated to be a point of unaffordability for families in this city of San Francisco and the entire bay area. Everything is being re-gentrified and causing normal neighborhoods to evict tenants who are now without affordable housing. Tragically, homelessness was becoming a growing problem in this city. This once beautiful city has fallen in disarray on so many levels; it is a travesty for this was once beautiful destination.

The "family" is becoming nonexistent in San Francisco. The idea of raising children in San Francisco is diminishing because families cannot afford to live in this city any longer, unless extremely wealthy. San Francisco was the city where my brothers and I were born. I was four years old when my family moved thirty miles south to Menlo Park and later, to the last family home built from the ground up in Cupertino, California, the birthplace of Apple, now known now as Silicon Valley.

Those simple ranch houses which my parents purchased in the early 1960s at $14,000.00, are now staggering multimillion dollars homes. You can find pictures of the replica of these structures from where Steve Jobs started the Apple Empire. They are not mansions, but simple ranch style homes, and small at that!

Coming from the simplicity of apricot and cherry orchards that surrounded our family homes, the produce industry once thrived from the Santa Clara Valley. Now the flourishing tech community have stolen the ability for families to live sustainably in this once quiet, sleepy valley or state, a generation of immense changes.

California's government has been taking down this state with a socialist bent of elected corruption not voted on by the people— another travesty of this time! Daily displays throughout the state of what unchecked socialism has brought upon the state. The death of a once thriving beautiful state is now the home of 50,000 homeless people in Los Angeles.

September 2015

I had taken trip to Texas to visit my daughter as preparation for my move out of California to be near my daughter and of course to establish my own life. I had started to pack before I left and though my spiritual son Nick was also helping while I was away, there was so much more to do. It was a lot to get done in such a short time.

I was planning to stay in Orange County for a while to make better preparations to make the move out of state but just before I arrived back in the area, I was advised that the place I was to stay would no longer be available. Doors were closing around me which shifted me to a place of huge uncertainty. With all of this on my return, yet another unexpected shift had happened. I got a call from my daughter who had now decided that her time for me to arrive there would not be for another four months. Clearly, I did not expect to be in the midst of this situation.

Continued Moving And Packing…

I had two additional days in the almost vacant apartment as I continued to pack and eliminate things that I was not carrying with me. I had sold or given away all of my furniture. Now, I muttered under my breath, *"where am I going?"* It hit me as I was about to turn in my key! I asked G-d, *"What are we doing? Where am I going?"* He said, *"You're going to be a sojourner for a season. You're going to see things through a different lens and you're going to become the message!"*

My next thought was, *"I haven't showered in two days, so I'll go to the gym, work out, shower and then go to Starbucks and study the Bible a bit and pray to listen and to hear what was next."* I went to the gym and showered first. At that point, I got a phone call from my friend Sandy asking where I was going to stay. I told her I didn't have a place as of yet, so she graciously invited me to come and stay with her for two days. This was my first miracle! I had been contemplating sleeping in my car that night in the gym's parking lot if necessary. I was of course, enormously grateful! But G-d was going to be my compass and truly my provision for many days yet to come.

Mission Bay Beach Communit: San Diego, California

The next few days, my friend Debbie, who has a rental home and an attached apartment in the Mission Bay area of San Diego, offered me a vacant apartment for one week. I brought all of my paperwork and spent the week organizing years of paperwork and putting it all in good order! I would then take it to storage.

Meeting A Long-Term Displaced Senior

It was here I met another friend of Debbie's staying there in the main house; her name was Barbara. I was about to hear her unusual story.

Debbie had also come down from Orange County for a few days. We all had a few meals together and enjoyed the time we spent in each other's company talking and laughing. Being in the Bay area also allowed some nice walks through the city during the day. I didn't get to the gym as I had hoped, but these lovely walks on the Pacific Ocean beach were lovely.

It was still strange to be in this position. But the time here afforded me an opportunity to hear more of Barbara's story, and I was able to pour some encouragement into her life, as she too had a long history of unusual displacement. Barbara, also a senior, had been very wealthy but had lost everything through a grave accident on the job that ended with a debilitating physical injury.

Her story showed me how family and society could viciously turn on vulnerable people. This could not be happening when people are so much in need of compassion and assistance, could it? But this was also a testing time for Barbara since the tragic accident had depleted her. It is one of the greatest needs to be in a community and place that is safe for the young and the old as well. This is gradually diminishing with the insensitivity in broken family structures.

There has been a huge need to have a community that is committed to care and nurture thus facilitating physical and emotional healing. Such a facility could provide a resting place for one to be built up again and be released back into productivity. This was not the case with Barbara, and she weathered many storms. It took her years to recover from the disability that she incurred from the accident, and too many years of long, drawn out, unethical legal haggling which did not do justice for her pain and suffering. In the end, she was inadequately compensated in the settlement.

We need to nurture, honor and show respect for the strong character, values, and production in person's lifetime. One should peacefully retire in their senior years with all that has been worked through an individual who has prospered and prepared well.

Catastrophic things happen when faced with being unwell; there must be a hand of compassion. We need to be able to lean onto the stronger along the way and to aid in security when tragedy shift circumstances and before crises sets in.

"Two are better than one, because they have a good [more satisfying] reward for their labor; for if they fall, the one will lift up his fellow. But woe to him who is alone when he falls and has not another to lift him up! Again, if two lie down together, then they have warmth; but how can one be warm alone? And though a man might prevail against him who is alone, two will withstand him. A threefold cord is not quickly broken." (Ecclesiastes 4:9-12 AMPC)

Barbara, who had planned well, had a life of success and prosperity and owned several homes, but was shunned by loved ones because of that devastating physical accident which catapulted her into great losses. When I met her, she was very resourceful and resilient and was used to traveling often living out of her car with most of her needed possessions. She had some of her things in storage and access to places to stay for extended periods of time, but to say it was challenging would be an understatement. I admired her tenacity, fortitude and even the way she had a bar to hang her clothes on in her car. She looked lovely and very attractive that no one would consider her homeless at all!

In spite of all her challenges, she remained very cheerful, helpful and grateful. I am happy to report that after many years, she is doing very well and is in a very safe and cheerful place with friends and acquaintances who have now nurtured her from her past. They did not know her circumstances during this time. G-d is gracious and faithful! She now lives outside of California, encouraged by long term friends who have her back, and she is thriving in a state where the cost of living is more affordable than California!

Newport Beach Peninsula

I was grateful that my next location worked impeccably. A friend was renting a home on the Newport Beach Peninsula, and she and her son were going on a nice long, once in a lifetime trip to Israel and also to her home country of Turkey. She hadn't seen her family in years; this would introduce her teenage son to those he had never met. He was a product of having a single mother and no visible father figure, so to meet the family he never knew personally and the culture of the country his Armenian family fled from, would be amazing; clearly a wonderful thing for a young man of eighteen years of age.

They would be gone for a good amount of time, and I could stay in their home to take care of plants, pets, and the house. It was a win-win situation for me to have another secure place to stay as I tried to seek G-d more deeply and understand this new journey. I was studying and writing a lot and would be alone to ponder all that was ensuing.

It was during this time that I began to feel some stress and encountered some forms of fear considering my age and still not understanding the whole direction, purpose, and discovery of this journey. It was an extreme test of my faith and my identity. Little did I know that there were deep mysteries of my biological DNA that held me in captivity. It was a whirlwind of internal shaking as I tried to maintain a sense of purpose but not feeling completely connected internally. My emotions were shaky without the grounding of who I was to G-d. There were blockages as to how, what and why. My dauntless faith was sorely tested.

A spirit of torment hit me in regard to being sustainable. I didn't know its origins at that time, but later I was able to understand that there was a very deep need for biological DNA realignment. It had to do with my birth, the discovery of my biological heritage, the secrecy of who I really was and the losses of my culture! Whew, when G-d said I was going to see things through a different lens, I had no idea!

Revelations Of Our Historic Culture And Spiritual Roots

I was studying and learning so much and trying to connect the many dots. I was now being exposed to the false "Christian" path that has blinded many bearing this name of understanding the depth and the fabric of the hidden mysteries being released today. This is happening universally. It has never been more visible now that paganism and its practices have been woven into what we celebrated and believed as absolute truths, especially all the holidays we participate in. It's uncanny when we somehow sense that something isn't quite right.

It is here that I was introduced to a book called Santa-tizing by Robin Main, who had generously allowed me to study with her on the subject. Robin knew about my culture that was "hidden" from me and she was going to begin to give me some of the necessary tools. These helped to unlock to me many truths in this difficult season of the journey of "becoming the message".

"Santa-tizing" reveals the many rituals that are part of the celebration of "holidays" as we have known them to be to us. Many have been raised up in different cultures and the nations of the world. In Robin's book, she outlines different ages and where these traditions and rituals were added and adopted here and there. Oddly enough, we have never thought about the things we do in relation to celebrating those holidays. We blindly participate in them as our "traditions" year after year after year.

Even with the peculiarity of some of these different traditions, we have not been as widely challenged in the past. But today, we have felt the brunt of too much commercialism, and the truth is beginning to be revealed today during the times of celebration. They have been focused on the trappings of consumerism and not at all on what they represent. For example, Yeshua did not invent "Christmas." It is such a misguided event and has been built on so many falsehoods for centuries. We, as a western culture, adopted the Gregorian calendar have developed Christmas as a holiday along with its celebrations. Whereas, the Jewish people, have always celebrated and followed the Hebrew calendar and traditionally, always followed the biblical feasts, not the commercial holidays.

Many today are discovering that this was always the proper way and as we study this deeply, we realize we never should have left these spiritual truths. We can see that this has been another one of our losses and one of the great deceptions that we thought were culturally correct. But as truth and mysteries are on G-d's heart, we are perusing how the marriage of our historical and foundational truths are being presented and embraced today.

We are becoming unshackled as we delve deeply into our foundation that was stolen. From the time that Yeshua was on the earth, 325 years of undeniable supernatural living, that changed cultures until Emperor Constantine came into focus. Constantine ruthlessly altered the spiritual foundation and reinstituted a structured religious system and dismantled the power of the Hebrew people. Wow!

Engaging Ladybug In Newport Beach Peninsula, California: Where We Met

I begin to share in detail, my engagement with Ladybug, because she represented a visual and a physical representation of what is before us in the nations of the earth. Vulnerable human beings in devastating situations and needs—not just surface needs, but internal and external pain, and much disconnect from normal life. There is so much instability being addressed on a daily basis that it prevents the focusing on both the physical and the spiritual needs of humanity. We need to be sensitive to reach out wherever we can.

The Newport Beach Peninsula, California

So, while in Newport Beach Peninsula, California, I took care of two pets. Two furry friends, a tiny five lb. toy poodle named Lady and a cat named Faith. They loved and thrived on attention and were always around, especially at nights having one on each of my legs, just hanging around. It was a very funny experience.

In late September 2015, I was connected for the first time to the sweetest, little five pounds of JOY, with that precious little face. At that time, she was called "Lady," but I began to affectionately call her, *"my little Ladybug-bug—my little baby doggie!"* She was not a pup but a very fragile and nervous bundle of love, who just deeply needed to be nurtured!

Her former owner was going out of the country for over forty days and I was able to take care of her and her furry friend. Lady seemed to have some health issues from the get-go! Within days of my arrival she had a bout with diarrhea and because of her already very small frame, I was very concerned. I did not have information for a vet so I went to a pet store to see if I could gain some insight on her condition. I was given a very good brand of dog food specifically for toy breeds and after reading the label, I thought that I could eat it myself! She liked it! I now separated her food from the area where the cat ate hers. Just like humans, we have to be knowledgeable of the proper foods and what is in our food chain. This includes dogs and other pets too. Did you even think when pet food has different colors in it (which is food dye), that we are ingesting this?

With some coaxing, she began to enjoy the food, and the diarrhea stopped immediately! Now, I became very much aware of the importance of good dog nutrition. Ladybug's former owner had a busy lifestyle where pets were not the priority and thoughtlessly felt that combining dog and cat food into one bowl was a time saver; clearly not a good idea. I had never owned a dog, but I was now paying attention to the needs Ladybug.

I began to think about what the world would be like looking up from the perspective of being only five pounds. It would be daunting to be so low and at everyone's mercy from the ground up! Pretty intimidating at the very least! In Ladybug's case, I would engage her in two daily walks, all around the beach community where she lived at that time. She was a little skittish or would nervously look around to see if she could walk in a particular direction as if she would not be allowed to make the choice. I gave her complete permission to make that choice. There is great foliage in this beach community, and she could take her time to leisurely go with what suited her best, sniffing along the way! I gave her complete permission to choose the path we walked towards as any direction would offer her a good place to stroll.

She thrived on affection and human connectivity! It was a very sweet connection as she was so adorable! Needless to say, Both Ladybug and Faith slept with me every night! We all need to be loved and be in a warm community! And our furry friends need the connection just like humans do!

When Ladybug's owner returned from her trip, there was a bit of a difficult switch to Ladybug's routine. Currently, we are not sure whose routine was the difficult switch. I had treated her with a lot of affection during her owner's absence. She was always near me, either in my lap or sitting near my feet when I was on my computer studying or writing.

One of the exciting parts of her day was when I would prepare to walk her. She got very excited and literally jumped for joy to go outside! It was a big highlight to see how she loved and cherished the outside; don't we all love partaking in a beautiful day! This, apparently, had not been the norm for this little sweetie, and I was now disrupting the daily routine of the former owner's household. Now, we were relegated to rules and regulations which introduced separation! It was a bit over the top and I could see the sadness in this little girl with the encroachment on her time of being taken care of like any dear friend needs to be! After all, she is just a little dog, and that is how I was treating her; like a loving little dog!

As the days ensued, there were more household activity with people coming in and out. This is always great, but little Ladybug would retreat to me to be in a place of protection and of course, affection. This proved to be divisive and I was told not to interact with her at all How was this going to be possible? She is a dog! She thrived on the attention and nurturing. So many people need to be nurtured today. She modeled what is happening all around us so mindlessly. She felt protected with me.

"What the world needs now is love sweet love"

Ladybug's trauma and her attachment to me was being observed, and it got a bit out of hand while I was making designer holiday cupcakes late one night. Ladybug was now relegated to a little dog bed and was supposed to stay there. She looked so forlorn, as she popped her head over the top across the room and just looked at me. It was so pitiful! I thought the least I could do was to pull the little round bed close to the stool I was on, so I would not have to bear this sad little face! As I talked to her reassuringly and in a low voice, she barked!

Oh my gosh! Now the unthinkable happened! It had irritated her former owner who marched out of the bedroom and with an uncontrolled tug, pulled on this little round bed and flung it across the room with a strong force. It hit against the glass patio door, and Ladybug hit her head on the window!

My heart sank! I felt I had contributed to her harm by trying to comfort her! I am now the object of an emotional upheaval between this woman's difficult uncontrolled spirit and anger toward a very small vulnerable dog. Again, she is just a little dog, *a very tiny little dog!* It was so very hard to have been the one who brought about this sad expression of anger.

A Possible Income

Holiday bazaars became available at a moment's notice. Some possible income was presented. I've had this desire for a while and have dabbled in it in the recent past, but now I started to make what I called my *"girly girl"* cupcakes to see if I could start a stream of income. They were very ornate and looked a lot like pieces of jewelry and fun, but it took me a long time to learn a technique to produce them in very little time. I did two last-minute events but alas, no profit for my hard labors which was a bit disheartening. I had some great future contacts but feeling overwhelmed because it seemed I was striving and not spending enough time hearing G-d for the obvious— His plan in all of this.

But surely, He knew the disparity of my income and now 'rest' was leaving me in the lurch. I know that rest was the answer, but I felt a lot of pressure to produce income and I also know I had to vacate this location very soon.

Thanksgiving In America

I was invited to my dear friend Debbie's for Thanksgiving dinner. I had joined her family before for dinner on holidays and considering the circumstances at my temporary residence, it was nice to be in a warm family situation. My time was going to be up here soon, but my departure was going to take me to a place I had never been before. So, the tensions were high.

That day, I had received a call asking if it was possible for me to do cupcakes for a wedding. The wedding was in Beverley Hills and I would have loved the job, but at this point it would have been out of my league because I was still a novice. What a wonderful possibility! It warmed my heart to be considered!

A few nights later, lady's owner and some mutual friends of ours went out for dinner and a movie. Ladybug was now being relegated to the living room in her small round bed. The only light on was in the guest room where I sat on the floor, legs crossed working at my computer using a bench as a desk. Faith, the cat who roamed freely was in the room with me and before long, here comes little ladybug crawling into the room and sits in my lap as I continued to type. What was I supposed to do? She was in a dark room all by herself. What was I supposed to do? The dog is clearly being persecuted because of her need to be loved and cared for with affection.

Suddenly, the door opens leading to the garage, and the company of people had returned early from their night out. On the first sight of little Ladybug in my lap, all hell broke loose! It is astounding that one little dog could cause such a raucous! It was now at the point that I was chastised for being dishonoring to her requests.

Atmospheric Climatic Shifting

The next morning, the air was thick with resentment and emotion. I knew to keep things from escalating any more, that I should just go into the room I occupied and start packing my things. It was time to get ready to leave the premises. So, I calmly began to prepare to leave, not wanting to further the frustrations at hand.

The other guest, a friend of mine was also surprised and quite amazed at what was happening. Feeling the need to make an earlier departure, she also prepared to leave on an earlier train north. The air was uncomfortable, but there was a deep peace in my heart!

I already had a thank you card for the owner of Ladybug. I wrote, *"thank you for your hospitality, I am very sorry if you feel dishonored by me, it was not my intent. I hope you have a great holiday season."* and last but not at all the least, I asked her if I could bring Ladybug with me when I moved to Texas. After I took our mutual friend to the train, I returned to take my things and packed up the car to depart. When I arrived back at the house, she calmly agreed to let me take Ladybug to Texas when I left!

It must have resonated that she clearly didn't want the responsibility of a dog at this time in her life and knew it would be best for both of us. I took little Ladybug for the last walk I would take her on before I departed. Nearing the end of our walk I stopped and whispered in her ear, praying before temporarily returning her to her home. *"I pray for G-d to remove all traumas off you, all fear, anxiety, and stress! G-d loves you, and He will protect you! And I'm coming back to get you!"*

My First Time To Sleep In My Car

That night since the beginning of my journey, for the first time I had no place to go. Not knowing where I should go or how long this situation would last, I drove to my old neighborhood where I knew I would be safe, parked the car and walked around the local shopping center. Normally, I would have been tucked in comfortably at this time of the night at my former 55+ building just blocks from where I was.

It was now the last days of November, almost December which meant the weather was already cool. Though difficult to face at the beginning of this trail, the adventure this night was for me to walk around the many business shops into a large building that had been converted from a big box bookstore that had closed and reopened into smaller stores and restaurants called "pop-up" shops or businesses, I would later learn this was the escalating trend. This concept was ingenious to make business more affordable to brick-and-mortar start-ups—a new, growing concept.

Culturally, we have come to understand that many creative ideas being developed today is because of the different ways to modernize capitalism, thereby keeping the expenses lower in one common area by having a lot of small business enterprises in one larger location. It is really ingenious! We see the flow of our nation's sustainability shifting commerce. These ideas are amazing, but it is re-inventing and re-gentrifying old ways and the old models.

In this shopping center, there was a lovely seating area with contemporary outdoor furniture and an outdoor fireplace. I paused to warm myself, pondering the new circumstances and to stay up as long as possible before everything quieted around me. Another businesswoman, a widow, sat near me and we engaged in conversation as she waited to pick her son up from work. After we shared a little, I told her about my first book which was on prayer for businesses, and she asked me to pray for her; what a privilege!

Wholefoods Market had their doors wide open very late after business hours this particular night. There were a lot of trucks parked around the shopping center close to the entrance of the store. They were doing construction in the store during the long night hours. It was good for me to be safe there, so no one would be coming to get into a truck right away. I parked between two trucks, laid the seat down, pulled out a blanket and pulled it over my head. I went to sleep as best I could until the early hours of the morning. I woke up in time so as not to be conspicuous, folded up my blanket and tucked it away then went to the gym to clean up.

The parking lot would soon be empty of the trucks and would be vacant until the mid-morning shoppers arrived around 10:00 a.m. when everything starts buzzing. A single car parked there would draw attention.

December 4, 2015, Orange County California: Meeting The World Outside Of My Comfort -
My First Time Observing The Plight Of The Homeless Or Disenfranchised

I was in an area I would rarely even go, but there was a big Starbucks across the street from the place I had had a massage. And that is why I ended up there on this day for the free Wi-Fi. The music on the overhead speakers were so loud and it was placed right over the large table for people which was a common shared space for those using their computers. I asked for the music to be turned down once, but I felt as if I had been at a rock concert all day while I was there. So, I need earbuds or earplugs on this journey! You can't play any audio electronics without them and in the case of the loud music; one needs to be prepared to filter it out! A bit stressful at best but nevertheless, a place to write.

It was really interesting to observe. I stayed very late at this very noisy Starbucks and talked to a Loma Linda, (7th Day Adventist) college student sitting next to me at his computer. Earlier in day I had scheduled a Groupon massage that was still left in my account (which was paid for) but boy, did it make a difference! This had to be used, and it was nothing I had to pay for! The Asian woman, who worked on me, gave the best massage I have had in years! I left a good tip on a postdated check. I know I will have money in my bank account! She worked very hard on me. Because of all the hours I sat at the computer I even had cramps in my legs (which could be evidence of magnesium deficiency) but after the massage, I felt invigorated!

I took "calm" powered Mag before I left Los Angeles, but I think my body is not getting enough exercise! Ha, ha, that is an understatement! Not eating enough fruits and veggies at this time either, especially veggies! Nonetheless, this adventure was so interesting and revealing of the things going on in our society outside of normal living! We would never know.

The young man sitting next to me pointed out another young man who came and sat on the stool next to him. I was concentrating on what I was writing and had not noticed when he came in. He was dressed warmly. What I had noticed was how cold it was outside. You could feel the cold air rush in each time the door opened when someone came in or went out burr! I really needed a lap blanket; my knees were frozen!

The person on the stool was completely out of it, obviously on drugs of some sort and the young man to my right said, *"I wonder what he is on?"* It was so heartbreaking to see a human being so in bondage by the demonic influence of drugs and rendered ineffective for daily life. I'm sure the drugs were to deal with the obvious or the obvious was due to taking drugs. I would never have seen this sad situation being so far removed living in the posh Newport Beach community I had just left! There are so many people in need loving and healing! At any rate, these are things I've never been aware of before in my sheltered life.

As I continued sitting in Starbucks during earlier daylight, I continued working at my computer through the morning. At one point I looked up and noticed another young man in shorts and a light shirt, crouched down on a backpack outside the door. It seemed he just took a minute to rest. He was clean cut; not bothering anyone, but obviously homeless! A foot security officer came walking up, and it was obvious, the security was telling him to move on! So cruel! So, sobering out here! Seeing through new eyes for sure! The young man at the table told me that a lot of homeless people hang out in this area. I never would have thought so for this area and I would never have known this unless I had been out late. Orange County Homelessness!

Staying Out Later Than Usual As I Have Resorted To Sleeping In My Car

I left Starbucks and went to the gym at about 10:00 p.m. Not having a diligent, strong routine, I did a bit of a workout, swam and took a soak in the Jacuzzi. Needless to say, my butt, legs and shoulders were quite happy! A friend of mine had suggested I joined her in San Diego, but it would be a really far drive and I would need gas money to return to the Orange County area. So, I could not really fall asleep at the end of this day!

I had some trouble falling asleep and after driving around until past 2:00 a.m. I was hungry. Surprisingly, I found a Jack in the Box that was open and though not my normal diet, I got a breakfast burrito which was quite good. I found a safe, hidden place tucked away in my old neighborhood, but still did not sleep well and woke up at 4:44 a.m. The very hardest thing in this type of circumstance is the lack of a bathroom. It is something one does not think about. If you go to a gas station in the middle of the night, you can't just use a bathroom without a purchase. It is an unnerving problem. I pondered this for a just a bit as I packed up the car and drove to the gym to prepare for the day.

I talked to my friend Charlotte from Savannah, Georgia and asked her to continue to pray for me. I was starting to feel the effects of the lack of sleep last night and after picking up my mail at my P.O Box, I drove to a remote spot in the shopping center to try to get some rest.

Meeting Other Cultures At The Computer Table In Irvine: December 2016

In the middle of responding to a text my cell phone died and so I went into Coffee Bean and Tea to charge my phone and computer. I was at a large common table again where everyone sat to use their computers and I asked the woman on the other side of the table if she would watch my electronics while I used the restroom.

She graciously agreed and when I returned, I asked her about the book she was reading which initiated a very interesting conversation. I was in the process of meeting the most amazing young woman, who was kind enough to watch my stuff while I went to the bathroom. She is Muslim; a Pakistani by nationality and works in Los Angeles in Century City as a Legal Secretary. She lived here in Irvine and loved it but did not love Los Angeles, so this was a very long commute for her! But I can understand that the frequencies of cities are very different and not warm and fuzzy as Irvine. As she began to share with me, I was fascinated by her story. She spoke freely on many things including her Muslim background, what she felt about the attacks going on and the darker side (ISIS) of what was currently going on in the USA. She could not travel freely for a vacation at this time, so she had resigned herself to this as her "new normal." This was also the same for others in her age bracket and are legal immigrants. Rather alarming! She has reconciled herself to the plight of being Muslim in a time when she felt she would be profiled. So, it is better to not expose herself to this possibility to try to travel anywhere! What a sad concept and a true loss of freedom!

We had a delightful talk, sharing with me about her family. Her love for her family was palpable. She was in the same situation that my daughter had a year ago—a very long commute—which did not leave her much time for a very large social group! She said her circle of friends was very small *and* they were always so busy! This breeds a lot of loneliness and isolation! As one who raised my daughter as a single parent, I knew exactly how that isolation at times could feel.

She enthusiastically shared that, in spite of the long commute, she still chose to live in Irvine as it was a safe and lovely place. I understood that! I had lived in Irvine for many years because it has been known throughout the nation to be in the top five safest cities in the country. She had moved to Marina del Ray, very close to her job, but did not like the area at all and did not feel comfortable and safe there.

Irvine has always been one of the safest cities in America: *Here are some statistics Information on Irvine, California –*

Violent crimes per 100,000: 48.
Population: 235,830.
2013 murders: 2 (44th lowest).
Poverty rate: 12.1% (53rd lowest).
Pct. of adults with high school degree: 95.3% (7th highest).

Just 113 violent crimes were reported in Irvine in 2018, a city with more than 235,000 residents. The city's violent crime rate was just 48 per 100,000 people, the lowest among large U.S. cities. This would be the 10th straight year since date that Irvin has had the nation's lowest violent crime rate among large cities. Irvine's property crime rate was also extremely low, ranked ninth lowest in the nation. The city's consistent low crime rates are likely due, at least in part, to its high-earning and well-educated population. Last year, the median household income in Irvine was $87,830.00, and more than 61% of adults had at least, a bachelor's degree, both among the highest figures in the nation.

My new friend had also resigned to herself that she was past childbearing age, so why marry at all and it was obvious that Mr. wonderful had not arrived into her life at the moment. I said she could marry someone with children or adopt; it wasn't that cut and dried! It saddens me for so many young people to be so fatalistic without knowing the love of G-d's hope and plan for their lives. I do feel that people need community and to be connected, but it can be so elusive.

I took her email address, and I knew she had been refreshed and stimulated by our conversation. I shared as much as I could in the short time. But it was a G-d encounter to meet this lovely young woman. She didn't like what Dr. Ben Carson said about Muslims in general which I clearly understood. I told her that he was the first presidential candidate that addressed what we needed in our nation and that is common sense. A shift was needed because the current administration at that time and its party, have clearly lost their common sense regarding protecting our nation.

In the vein of radicalized Islam and ISIS, Dr. Ben Carson makes perfect sense. I am sure that if I was in her shoes, I would have to pause as well. I noted to her that Dr. Ben Carson and President Obama came from single parents' households, but their upbringing was polar opposites, being evidenced in who they became!

Finding Places With Wi-Fi To Write And Study During The Day

I felt it prudent to check out other Starbucks so I could have access to Wi-Fi during the day and went to one very close to my old neighborhood when I lived in Irvine before moving to Tustin. I needed to plug in my computer and keep it charged, but I had to wait for a space inside. While I waited, I sat at a table outside near the window. I went inside to look around just as someone was leaving and had to move quickly to secure the table.

My friend Karen had given me a book which I had placed on the table when I was waiting for a table inside. Apparently, through the window, this gentleman had seen the book and he asked me about it. I told him that the book was about a man who had died in a plane crash and went to heaven and how Karen's husband, a movie producer planned to make the book into a movie and Karen had asked that I read the book and pray for the project.

We were having a really nice dialogue. and I told him that I was also writing a book chronicling my adventures. He then asked me if I knew the other gentleman who was also writing a book and came to this particular Starbucks as well. Starbucks seemed to be a haven for writers!

I transitioned my things to the table inside, and during our conversation, I learned that this man was a Muslim who was on business training here in the USA. He seemed to have an interest in different types of Christian literature. He introduced me to other author, Mike, from New York and a meeting was scheduled between him and me. Mike was researching and writing about the human condition and the loss of affordable housing everywhere. This topic is clearly one that many are noticing and seeing that it needs to be addressed.

Late Night Starbucks In The Tustin Shopping Center

I was headed to the gym this particular night in Tustin but thought it was a bit early. Going a bit later would be better for me because I would need to come out into the night alone after the gym and find a safe place in this neighborhood without looking conspicuous.

In Tustin, I chose a Starbucks not far from where I had recently lived. I decided to put my computer on a bar next to the window and sit on a stool next to a beautiful, young Asian woman. She sat down next to me. She had headphones and stood up and asked if I could watch her space and her computer as she went to the restroom. I couldn't help but notice the information on her computer screen showed that she was listening to Christian music. We struck up a great conversation and I found out she was majoring in business. I told her about my original book, written on prayer for business and finance and she was very interested. She confided in me her about the needs in her family, school, and funds to continue her education.

It is not easy paying for education today. It is extremely expensive, and a large percentage of students graduate with an exorbitant amount of debt. This young woman was a solid believer with a strong prayer life. I know we were to meet as she truly needed some encouragement. The appointment had been set before we ever met. We prepared to leave and went outside—it was quite late now—I was able to pray with her. She later texted me to let me know she had ordered the book. I knew G-d would speak to her through the book.

Again, this is an amazing opportunity to be a quasi-evangelist exhorter and cheerleader along the path of this sojourner's experience, and clearly, the appointments are being made daily. It was getting late and I was tired and just needed to find a safe place to retire for the night. It has been very fatiguing not to have a permanent place to rest. But surely, there are many who are in a really difficult place more vulnerable than I.

I am learning that there is such a need to work on these gaps of human dignity to improve the situations. These times of transitions of those in more vulnerable experiences need to be made known. We face many fundamental human needs in such a very prosperous area that is not known for this type of difficulty. I am definitely seeing things through very different lens.

Helping A Single Mom

This is an exciting new daily adventure without a lot of definitive plans, but G-d orchestrates it all! I had some cupcakes that needed to be delivered to my friend in Burbank and was able to stay there for a few days. While there, I arranged to meet with a young lady, a single mom who have seen a lot of tragedy in her young life. Her husband who had a drug addiction committed suicide at a very young age by walking off a rooftop in San Francisco. Her son who had tried to commit suicide in the past year had also gone through brain surgery and was coming out of medical rehab. The trauma of both these events coupled with the thought of losing her son was devastating.

She was now assisting him to enroll in Los Angeles International Churches, Dream Center's discipleship program. The Dream Center is a multiservice Christian organization in Los Angeles, California with a yearlong discipleship program. It would be the frosting on the cake to expedite emotional healing and building up a spiritual foundation. So many people were praying for this young man. He was about to be restored and completely changed. He was going to come out in an amazing state as a complete miracle.

As it turned out, she was an Uber driver and asked me if I could help her out. She asked me to sign up as an Uber driver under her code in December because if I did and completed twenty rides, she would receive a $350.00 bonus. This would really bless her. In addition to what wages I made, I would also get another bonus of $150.00. Of course, there were stipulations which included good car insurance, a car model that met Uber's criterion that was in good condition and would need to pass Uber inspection. So, I met with my mechanic in Glendale who did a few cosmetic things that needed to be done anyway, checked a few other things and I was ready to go.

Getting the car inspected and passing the Uber testing would not be completed until December 18, so it was necessary for me to remain in Orange County. Although offers to stay with other friends were available, I had limited funds and the cost to drive back and forth to Los Angeles, I would need to stay in my car a few more days. This was something I was really waiting for — some cash flow and I needed to get my car insurance renewed. It was so obvious G-d had provided this and was guiding my steps to help a single mom as well.

Fortunately, my friend Stephaney had a lovely friend Doris, who lived in the Garden Grove area. Doris was kind enough to give me a weeks' worth of accommodations for the start of this Uber journey. Doris had assisted women in situations like mine before, so it was an enormous blessing to be with someone who knew the challenges and truly knew how to embrace a sojourner. It was wonderful to experience what we all take for granted. From the last five days of no place to stay, I now have a lovely guest room and a bed to come to. One really learns to appreciate a home environment, and I was so grateful after those five days of sleeping in my car.

I started to drive for Uber on the 18th of December and did thirty rides in the first two days. It was rather exhilarating meeting so many different kinds of people with so many stories. I would ask an extraordinary question to everyone. "So, *what is your passion?"* And then it would flow from there, a flood of information captured in a moment in time with a complete stranger, one of G-d's creations.

I quickly accomplished my mission! I even exceeded the requirement by ten rides, so this single mom was able to receive her bonus quickly. I would receive mine at the end of the week's tally. This seemed like a million dollars to me at this time. A little income was very welcome now. The first check was not that large because I would have to figure out a rhythm of what hours to drive, the best locations and traffic flows, so I could earn the best income. There was also the cost of gas and the car had to be impeccably clean each day. Uber prided themselves on being a no-tips necessary business, but the driver had to pay for gas daily as well as the car had to be impeccably clean each day. I spent time studying and watching successful Uber drivers' YouTube videos to learn the business for a novice like me to make the most money possible.

It was an amazing, mesmerizing business; a whirlwind of being called all over and literally meeting the "world". Of course, I started in my neighborhood of Orange County and ended my last client all the way up by the Long Beach airport very near to where Doris's home was located. The Christmas holidays came and since I had no family in California to celebrate it with, Doris was kind and fixed a little meal that we enjoyed together. She also accommodated me with a little cash to keep the gas tank filled, an obvious necessity for a driver.

I had never worked so hard for so little in my entire life. The work was tiring but it was bringing some revenue. I was seeing many parts of this area of Southern California that I had never been in or knew existed. Even though I had lived there for a very long time, it was an education on many levels. I suppose with an upgraded car, one could probably make decent money doing this job, but it would be hard work.

I prayed a lot when driving and knew many of the areas. Each day, the rides I picked up were the people who truly needed a spiritual reality. Two clients stood out for me now as I reminisce at this point of writing. One seems to have been a high-level motivational speaker and businessman. the Uber call was in the canyons of Beverley Hills above the city. I was not given an exact address, so I texted the number and he came out somewhere mid-street and hopped into the front seat. He needed to go to Los Angeles Airport.

Sometimes, it seemed odd to have celebrities in an unsophisticated small Uber when they could afford a nicer higher priced Uber or a town car. But I felt I had an assignment and prayed quietly over them all without exception. I took the back roads to the airport, which was the fastest route and to my surprise, he was unfamiliar with that route. It got him to the airport on time where he was met by a representative to greet him upon his arrival at the airport to ensure he was provided with VIP treatment for his seating and his flight. Before each client exits the car, I always ask *"did you get everything?"* to which he replied *"yes"* as he got out of the car and then he left. At the end of my driving for the day, I found he had left a baseball cap on the floor of the front seat area. Written on it were these words: *"It's Lonely at the Top."* Wow! So very revealing. I called it in for him to have it delivered to him but did not receive a response; very interesting.

The next person I remember vividly was client I picked up in West Hollywood on a Friday night in an area where a man might be looking for a man as a date or a connection. He was so inebriated; he was almost unable to communicate with me. Because I had the habit of asking people what their passion was, I found out that he was an ER Doctor and he lived close to Cedars, a very big, well-respected hospital in this area.

My heart ached for him because I could sense such loneliness and the need to be loved. As we neared where I would drop him off, I grabbed his arm and spoke into his life. I simply said, *"You are very important, and people need you and what you do. Please don't drink. You have a very necessary position to help people in crises."* I just had to say something that would speak into his spirit. As I watched him maneuvering and weaving his way to his door, I just began to weep.

Everyone wants to feel loved and be significant on this earth. He was among so many looking to be loved. Rarely can this be satisfied with brief encounters because that doesn't allow for true intimacy. I met so many, many people with all kinds of needs and issues as I drove around the southern California basin. I did this for a total of seven weeks before I left California. Had I not been an Uber driver, I would never have seen these lives nor had the opportunity to silently pray into their circumstances. What an experience; truly another part of the sojourner revelations.

The reality of the human condition is seeing, entertaining and entangling with many lives with so many different realities and perspectives. There were so many stories in a society that is not really connected. Many successful people, movers and shakers, are just longing for companionship. Many are just working hard with no wife, children and family.

One girl was so sick, I had to stop the car for her because she had to vomit, and she could not rule out pregnancy. I encouraged her to be sober minded about her choices if this was the condition. I knew that in a time like this, hidden agendas have very long-term consequences and even depression may ensue at a great magnitude. False intimacy is sold as an instant convenience. It grieves me to see what has become of the sacredness of human life.

Moving To The Beverly Hills Guest House

It was almost humorous to be moving to Beverly Hills where I had worked for so many years and even lived there for a while when I was young. My friend invited me to stay in their guest house, and I knew that this shift would have me now driving in the Los Angeles area. I arrived the day Christmas knowing that my time here would be on my own because the family had very busy lives. It was another sojourners accommodation and the hand of G-d provided for this last part of the journey in California.

Receiving Ladybug; Never To Be Separated Again!

As for my dear little Ladybug, it was the second week of January when I got the call that would reunite us. It was a short conversation, *"I'm moving next Saturday, come and get Lady on Friday;"* direct and to the point. Thank G-d it was a flexible day for me! I was now temporarily staying with friends in Beverly Hills, so I ran my errands all the way south to Orange County on Friday. On the way to pick up Ladybug, the first thing I did was stop at a PetSmart and purchased a bag of the healthy dog food made specifically for Toy breeds. No gross food coloring, just good nutrition specific to her needs.

Now, we could begin the journey to health and wellness with the proper food first! The next thing I picked out was what is called a "bra" harness, in baby pink, one to go around her body and to properly clip to a leash that was *not* around her neck. It had tortured me to see her pulled and walk with a collar around her neck and without a retractable leash! These were our mainstays immediately needed!

When I picked up Ladybug, I put her in her little round bed in the passenger seat so she could be near to me. I was leaving for Texas on

January 31st, so she was booked on the flight with me. We were starting a new chapter as sojourner companions! She was now my little dog and sweet charge! She was now safe to be properly cared for with no more confusion! She would no longer be banished to a large pillow on the floor in the bedroom moving to the farthest corner to feel secure. She was now free to feel warmth and have additional blankets cover her in the winter nights! She was now FREE to receive unconditional love without boundaries!

Taking Ladybug For A Walk In The Park

I took Ladybug for an early morning walk in Will Rogers Park which was close to where we were staying and right across the street from the grand Beverly Hills Hotel, fondly known as the "pink palace." I had worked in the salon there many years before when I was in the beauty business. Coincidentally, I came to find out that a small group of people met up there on a daily basis to walk their dogs. One of the gentlemen gave me a name of a vet and a groomer he highly recommended, noting their affordability.

I found out that Ladybug had never had her shots which made it difficult to get her groomed because she couldn't be groomed without them. She hadn't been groomed in four months. I could hardly see her eyes and her nails needed to be trimmed so badly she was constantly slipping on the hardwood floor. She was so tangled, she had to be completely shaved and the weather wasn't even warm, brrr! How I hated to have to do that to her!

The groomer gave her the cutest little Japanese teddy bear cut and with her adorable face and two little hot pink bows – that added much greater cuteness! She looked really sweet and happier! The vet's comments were the alarming part, stating that shots were the least of her problems as she was too skinny and dehydrated—poor little thing. So, the first thing was hydration! I was relieved that her blood work and fecal tests were good, but she would still need rabies shots. We had gotten her a good vet here and she was now good to fly to Texas. The only remaining health issue now was a big one, her teeth. She had bad breath and dogs need to have their teeth scaled so this bill would also be a big one!

After hydration, she was a lot better and she was eating her food well. No more dyed colored cat food mixed with what she ate! And no gluten in the food as filler (thank G-d)! Her bill will be $400.00 to $500.00 here in California!

When I had to board her for several days to attend some meetings, they gave her antibiotics to help the preparation. She is now caught up on her shots. She is much healthier dog now; loved, accommodated and cared for. I am so grateful our lives intersected when they did. She will now be a part of our new moves to assist humans with a lot of needs who we will encounter along the way. She will be a part of assisting in unburdening some of the difficulties they may be experiencing. So much is in the works through this little girl's sweetness, and she is a magnet to all those around her. She is like a personal calling card as they stop to love on her and enjoy how adorable she is. Who knew that one little tiny dog could inspire others!

California - The Last Week Of January 2016

It was about 4:00 p.m., and I was driving down Santa Monica Blvd on Friday night, January 29th, 2016 in bumper-to-bumper traffic. I wanted to get a retractable leash for Ladybug and she and I headed east in hopes of finding a store where I could purchase one. The cars were going oh-so-slow because of course, this is normal, Friday night Los Angeles traffic! All of a sudden, bam! I had hit a business utility truck in front of me puncturing my radiator! Looks like shopping is on hold and this is a bit of a mess given I am leaving for Texas on January 31st! The car is supposed to be shipped there! What a mess!

It was a very long wait for the tow truck, which came all the way from the Valley. This only happens in Los Angeles; to bring a tow truck from a far distance. The location of the accident was just a little way past West Hollywood going east! The accident happened at 4:30 p.m. and the tow truck came at 8:30 p.m. So, you can imagine the weekend traffic if you know L.A at all! It was going to be very slow!

My mechanic and auto body person Aram, an Armenian man, stayed late on Friday night to wait for the car to be towed to his service garage. He is one of the kindest men I know and giving to a fault! He has always accommodated me in other crises.

It is a city well known for this large community of Armenians! If you need a mechanic, body shop, tires and anything else related to car needs, these Armenian men are excellent and go the extra mile in service. The place is PRO Automotive 1900 Flower Street Glendale, California, so I highly recommend HIM and his crew. He really needs to expand and take the whole block and own it! He is that respected and busy!

The transport from the towing pickup was well past the time to get a rental car. So, I stayed overnight on the night of the accident (along with Ladybug) at a friend's nearby. We didn't even get picked up by towing until about 8:30 p.m., the night of the accident! If you know Santa Monica Blvd and Los Angeles traffic on Friday night, you know nothing moves fast! (An interesting side note, the towing driver, was Armenian as well!)

I had to ask my dear friend Stephany and her friend Philippa who lived in Burbank if Ladybug and I could spend the night. I was fortunate that they were not far from Aram's garage in Glendale. The next morning (Saturday), I would need to pick up a rental car to drive to Irvine to the storage space to meet the moving van.

My Last Night In My Home State Of California: Leaving From The City Of Beverly Hills

Well, it's surreal leaving California, having lived in this state my entire life, especially now that I am leaving from the city of Beverly Hills! This was the city where I came to work as a hairdresser at age 22, just south of Wilshire Blvd. on South Beverly Drive between Gregory Way and Charlieville.

G-d is interesting! I had spent my last seven weeks living in my dear friend's guest house in Beverly Hills. I would go out early each morning for breakfast keeping track of all the many necessary details that I needed to do, to make my soon exit to Texas. I stayed pretty busy with all that had to be done before I would leave the city to go to work driving for Uber.

I had one more evening here in this town, so I decided to take Ladybug downtown for a little walk and a stop at Coffee Tea and Bean to just have a coffee, sit and ponder on the ensuing shift and how my life was formed on this very street just doors away, so many, many years ago!

As I drove south on Beverly Drive, I was at a stop light and directly to my right, I noticed a young man sitting on a bench in front of *IL*

Fornaio Restaurant, which is a popular moderately priced Italian restaurant. It has great food. He got my attention as I pondered on him quickly. He had a short beard, wore a hoodie sweatshirt, his hands were in his pockets but from what I could see, they were black from grime. He looked straight ahead with a somewhat blank stare, and a stab went through my heart instantly! I said,

"Oh G-d, nobody sees him, he's completely invisible to the many Friday night people, going about their weekend evening, enjoying a night out with friends and family! G-d, he's probably really hungry. Perhaps, he sat there thinking someone would see him and buy him dinner."

The light quickly changed, and I had to move on. I simply said, *"G-d what do you want me to do?!"* I continued down Beverly Drive and turned down Gregory Way and parked my car, taking Ladybug in tow. We walked North on Beverly Drive until we came to the Coffee Tea and Bean. We went inside, got a coffee and sat outside with others and watched the people maneuvering up and down the Boulevard. My thoughts were many, and I was now about through with my coffee and about to get up and go. I took a quick look to my direct right and shockingly, within a few feet of me, was the very same young man I had seen several blocks away at the stop light on North Beverly Drive!

To my horror, he was rummaging through the garbage can, and nobody paid attention or noticed him. He reluctantly walked away with nothing, as he headed north again on Beverly Drive! I couldn't stand it any longer! He is really hungry, and G-d had set this up by sending him right in front of me. It was now my duty to respond! I gathered my things and walked in the same direction he did hoping to find him quickly! Fortunately, he was just a few doors north and stopped to lean on a metal bar outside of a building. I got face to face with him and said, *"What do you want for dinner?"* He could have said anything; I would buy whatever he wanted. He simply said, *"a subway sandwich."* I asked him to lead me there and we walked down a few blocks to the Subway. I asked the lady behind the counter to give him whatever he would like, and I would pay for it. His order was simple. He took the food and walked out into the night.

The long and late evenings of driving all over Los Angeles took its toll and I was so exhausted, I had little else to give him. He was one of the first personal interactions with young homeless people. That night is forever etched in my mind.

The throw-away society is a human society, strongly influenced by consumerism. The term describes a critical view of overconsumption and excessive production of short-lived or disposable items, over durable goods that can be repaired. It seems to be happening with young people a lot. I don't know the young man's circumstances; he looked to be in his late 30s. But young adults who have no mentors, or who get aged out of foster care, have no role models or the ability for them to have adequate provision to even consider the proper sustainability. This is a reality in today's world. The nuclear family is not always one's reality. All I could do was to meet tonight's need, but where is he now?

With all that ensued on the night before with my auto accident, I still had a rush to get my final things done. I told him that I would be praying for him. I wish I had more on me and that I was filled up with G-d's touch to really speak some hope into his circumstances. But the encounter was a moment in time when we pay attention to the things around us!

I know it was no accident that we intersected that night. He is G-d's creation, and we are sometimes so oblivious to the great needs that call for our attention on our daily scroll of destiny. Being disenfranchised is a plight in society today and it could take so little effort to reach out and get to the core of the human condition.

It was such a young age for one to not have vitality and hope in his life! I'll never forget him, and I do pray that somehow, somewhere, G-d does reach him, and his circumstances are dramatically changed forever. I thank G-d that He allowed me to have eyes to see and to be used in a very basic way to reach out where some were just too busy with a life of comfort and ease to bother. Inconvenience has eroded and desensitized the blatant human condition.

"The King will reply, 'Truly I tell you, whatever you did for one of the least of these brothers and sisters of mine, you did for me.'"
(Matthew 25:50 New International Version NIV)

The sad condition of our human frailties! In the process of writing this book, housing costs has peeked into a national crisis. In my research, I have found out this is happening in other countries. The out-workings of corruption in government and the horror of Agenda 21 is demonized control of a nation that is becoming insensitive to the plight of the human condition. We all have a part to play in rebuilding communities around us.

The Former Beverly Hills Hotel Pool Manager: Homeless At Age 87

This story surfaced in 2017, a year after I left the Beverly Hills area. I worked in the historic Beverly Hills Hotel beauty salon in the '80s so it was very alarming to read this story. This man lost his home to some unscrupulous real estate deal, and from there, everything declined for him. It's a story of riches to rags for the former Beverly Hills Hotel pool manager who is now struggling to get by after decades of being surrounded by the rich and famous.

Svend Peterson was now using a walker and living in his car. Through the compassion of many who heard his story, including popular American actress Sandra Bullock, a fund was started for him. You can view his story on YouTube.

Sandra Bullock, the popular American actress, started the awareness of his needs by giving $5,000.00 to the funds which were raised for him. Although it states in the article that he is homeless, people who assisted the fundraiser for him, managed it, got him a nice apartment and furnished it. So, to this date, he is safely attended to and taken care of.

Here is some of his published story: Svend Petersen, the man once dubbed "The Poolside Prince", is now homeless after losing his money in bad real estate deals, and recently took to YouTube to make a sobering plea for help. For years, Petersen, now 86, presided over the pool at the posh hotel, which served as the hangout for some of the most glamorous stars in show business.

"Do not rebuke an older man but encourage him as you would a father, younger men as brothers, (1 Timothy 5:1 ESV)

"You shall stand up before the gray head and honor the face of an old man, and you shall fear your G-d: I am the Lord" (Leviticus 19:32 ESV)

"Do not cast me off in the time of old age; forsake me not when my strength is spent." (Psalm 71:9 ESV)

We never had these experiences years ago, but they are real today. We simply must do our part today in a shifting economic culture for so many!

Back In Orange County For My Last Night

I got up the next early morning to say my goodbyes to my dear friends who had allowed me to stay in their guest house for several weeks in Beverly Hills. They generously also helped in sponsoring my trip out of California. I am forever grateful for the tremendous kindnesses that this family is known for. They have been generous to a fault to me and my family over many years. Being in the safety of their guest house afforded me the ability to work for the last seven weeks in the Los Angeles area. It allowed me to assist this single mother make her bonus and to continue to fund the daily needs and expenses for Ladybug to join me.

I now had to head south in one hour or more to the storage space in Irvine, to meet the moving van. My niece and nephew were going to assist me in sorting out the rest of my things to be shipped to Texas. The movers would be there by 11:00 a.m. to load up the moving van from my small 5x5 unit. This would then forever close the chapter of my twenty-four years living in Orange County, the seventeen years in the city of Irvine and the last four in Tustin! And I would leave the state that I was born and have lived in my entire life.

Saying Goodbye To A Few Friends

The week had been packed and even though I worked evenings and nights, I wanted to extend a casual invitation to many of the dear long-term friends who could join with me to say goodbye and connect with each other. It was a sweet "spur of the moment" to have a simple meal and say good-bye!

I invited about twenty people, but the group was a bit cozier, a really nice group of people who had been so kind to me on so many levels and whom I had met and interacted with in many ways! They generously blessed me with a little money, and it was just fun, fellowship and a good feeling saying goodbye!

In the morning, Ladybug and I were fortunate to have a smooth departure, leaving my nephew's home early to catch the plane. He accommodated me by having the car ready, a little breakfast in hand, and all my things tossed into the car, even backing the car up to load. What a gentleman!

We were off to return the rental car at the Enterprise car rental, and I was a bit concerned, as I had two suitcases, a dog carrier, a computer, another packaged computer. How was I going to return the rental car and get everything on the shuttle? Then with all of this focus at hand, and driving into the airport, would I get a great skycap that would seamlessly help me to the checkout counter? It went amazingly well; the skycap got everything on board immediately and took me right to the ticket stand. I tipped him big! Whew, we are on our way.

Texas, Here I Come: January 31, 2016, Arriving At Dalla, Fort-Worth Airport

A dear friend kindly agreed to pick me up at the airport and helped me book an Airbnb in the Fort Worth area. In February there was going to be a large conference with very influential leaders and so it made sense that I stayed in Fort Worth. Ladybug weathered her first airline flight very well; she is a little trooper!

The neighborhood was very different from where we were in California, but the Airbnb accommodations were perfect for the days we would be there. All the activity of the days before including the car accident made me completely exhausted. My car would be shipped to a yet undisclosed location so for now I was without transportation.

For the next two or three days, I was so exhausted I slept for most of the day and left the room only to take Ladybug for walks. I had no appetite for food and ate very little of the "snack-breakfast" they provided. I needed rest!

I had been without Wi-fi for the past seven weeks and was excited for the convenience and the opportunity to finally be able to check emails. A Pinterest email with an article on designing ladybug cakes, cake pops and cookies caught my attention. I was inspired and immediately started to research cake pops as a Ladybug Loves product. I could really develop this as a thriving business in the cottage industry. Though rules change from state to state, Texas had the very best cottage laws and are huge supporters of small businesses.

There were not grocery stores nearby and only one fast food place across the street, so we ventured out to see what else was in the neighborhood. We turned down one of the streets, I glanced down and there on the sidewalk right in front of me was *a little ladybug walking across my path*! I stood in silence for a moment, my eyes stinging from the tears that filled my eyes!

Fort Worth, I would find, was being gentrified as was a lot of Texas. The area in which we found a Target store was a conglomerate of a few big box stores and new condos and businesses built below. It was a very exciting area to begin to explore. We later got to see a bit more on public transportation. I was to find a lot of the old and new Texas all around. Fort Worth was on the rise.

I hated leaving as it was ideal for the time being. We left our luggage there as we walked to get a new phone cord for our phone. The Airbnb had prior bookings and though it was ideal, we had to book other accommodations. It was hard finding another Airbnb that was affordable could accommodate a long block of time, so we booked into a hotel for a time. We eventually found a great Airbnb which was more like a studio apartment. The owners, a lovely young couple adored Ladybug. Dogs are much loved and accommodated here in Texas for which we are very happy. The only problem we encountered was the nights here was very cold and there were no extra warm blankets. We had to bundle up. We were not used to the cold at all. Brr!

The owner of the Airbnb and her mother was very gracious and took us to Hobby Lobby, a store known for everything that pertains to home-based businesses, artistic talent and of course, hobbies. I was able to use their discount to purchase the products needed to start the Ladybug Love products. We were so very blessed! Our next adventure would be to travel to Dallas for a day.

Dallas: Easy Storage On S. Haskell, Meeting Javier In person.

I paid in advance for a Texas storage space before I arrived, so that I would have a location to ship my belongings to. I shipped the things I retained and would still need or things which I didn't sell or give away. They were now arriving. Not having access to transportation and not really knowing the area, I hired an Uber driver and headed out to meet the moving van.

Javier, the young man who helped me book the storage space was so polite he made a great impression on me. When I arrived, he was on the phone, so I took Ladybug for a quick walk do her business. All of a sudden, I heard a voice on a loudspeaker shouting, *"Free showers, then breakfast and then Bible study."* I looked in the direction where the voice was coming from and I was shocked! Of all the storage places that are in Dallas, Texas, I was in one across the street from a ministry that reached out to the homeless population! Incredible! We wandered on to a large patch of grass and stood beside a chain linked fence. I heard a dog bark and followed the sound. There before me was a whole tent city on the other side of the fence; a homeless encampment. I was stunned and undone. Coincidence? No, just another tug in my heart of what G-d was allowing me to see, the human condition up close and personal.

Back inside the office, Javier was off the phone and we greeted each other. I was about to hear his remarkable story as we waited for the soon arriving moving truck. Moving often has a lot of drama that one cannot possibly foresee. Today was going to be one of those days. It seemed like G-d made sure that Javier and I had plenty of time to talk and visit as the calls and walk-ins were scarce.

I began to hear his amazing story. He had done three tours of duty in the military, and he saved a buddy's life, carrying him to safety. He had this position for six months! He was very polite, and one could tell he was an excellent worker. He took his job seriously and was a model employee. His manager was on vacation, so he should be really inundated at this time, but G-d allowed us a long visit! His mom left the family when he was twelve, and he took a parental role helping to raise his younger brothers. He couldn't say enough about his father and what a good role model he was! He too, is now in a relationship with a young lady who has two sons that are not his biological children. During our conversation, I was able to speak to him on a variety of topics. Most emphatically, how much he was loved by G-d. I could see the tears, and he said, *"I'm going to cry."* I knew this was going to be an ongoing friendship and it was not by chance we were meeting today.

Corrupt Moving And Storage Van Businesses

The moving van finally arrived, and I was to better understand the reason for the frenzied calls the day before. When buying the shipping package, the salesperson did a great job of not highlighting important details until the service is sold. Don't these people understand when working within a tight budget that every dollar count!

The first time I met with the movers from the shipping company in California, there were a few red flags. I was on my way to the storage to meet my niece and nephew who were going to help me with a few things to be ready for when the moving truck arrived. I received a call from the moving company at 8:30 a.m. to let me know they were already there and waiting. They were not expected until 11:00 a.m. Great, now we had to work with their schedule. This would be my first lesson in understanding the corruption in this industry and more would follow in Texas.

Once the movers finished, they calculated an amount that was way different than what I was told previously. I had already made a down payment by check so that couldn't change and because I had not been able to read the last few emails, there were more unexpected changes. The way payment is made in this industry is first, a deposit. I guess this is supposed to ensure that you are locked in. The movers suggested that I paid the rest in cash, money order or a cashier's check – I chose the latter! There would also be a 15% gratuity because this is considered a service industry; so, an additional $180.00 increase in the cost that was not budgeted for. This was embarrassing!

Now at this end, different drama, but the lesson continued. As soon as the driver called, he asked to be sent a picture of the cashier's check so he can complete the delivery at this end. I sent the picture to him and soon received a call from a company employee in a panic now saying that I can only pay by cash or money order! I emphatically stated this is what I was told, and it will be the only way the driver will be paid. The lady I spoke with calmed down after she saw I would not budge or be intimidated! Whew, now we will see where G-d is amazing and so good! The deception in this industry is, they think that they can be greedy by not informing people that there will always be "hidden costs" that will be imposed on their end.

I was told I had to give the driver the check before he unloaded, fair enough. Javier took him to a rented 5X5 unit and after some time they came back with the driver noting that the space was too small and would not hold everything. I adamantly said, *"Oh no! You are wrong, it is all going in! There was only one item that was not in the 5X5 in California and that should not be a problem!"* He then made another attempt at intimidation, *"I measured the distance from the moving van* *to the rented unit and this will cost you $400.00 more,"* to which I calmly replied, *"no it won't."* He then threatens not to release my things!

Javier now jumps in; he goes through the available spaces on his schedule. After observing the closest unrented space near the entrance where my things were to be unloaded, he tells the man and his two local helpers that they can unload into an available free space. The limits that were imposed were now dealt with, and there will be *no* additional fees for me! This was done seamlessly, I signed off on the delivery after everything was unloaded. After they had left, for the next two hours, Javier moved all my stuff into the 5X5 storage space I had rented. If Javier had not been there, I could not have done this by myself.

G-d will *not* let unethical people steal from His children. And He now has established a new spiritual foundation in Javier's life. The time I spent with him was invaluable in sharing the things of G-d, and this will *not* be our last encounter. He is a pre-manifest son of G-d and G-d blesses those who are kind and gives selflessly, and Javier is that young man! He will go far in life because G-d had us cross paths today.

My whole five-month journey up until this point was to encounter the people with no religious affiliation, but just needed to be loved. It was evident that I had a whole new love for them; they are the heart of G-d!

My friend, G-d is not waiting for you to meet the people so you can be a house of refuge at some time later down the line. They are right in front of you today! I love the people who have no spiritual foundation as I desire this as my inheritance! I am having the time of my life meeting people. I would never have met any of them if G-d did not provide this journey of the sojourner! I am so honored to meet them. *"Thank you, G-d, for allowing me to be used in their lives!"*

My stay was now over here in this Airbnb, so I moved again, this time to an extended Stay America hotel in Fort Worth in a beautiful neighborhood not much different than Southern California with other hotels and shopping centers.

Texas, South Fort Worth: Sunday, February 14; My Car Arrives

I was now in Texas for fifteen days. I got a call from the driver of the transport truck who was shipping my car from California to Texas. He said the delivery would be on Sunday. On our next call, after giving him the delivery location the day before, he said. *"I will be there in a half an hour!"* Wow, to be in a place for fifteen days and having stayed in several places and not even knowing where you really are is very strange!

I was expecting the driver in half an hour and Ladybug needed to be taken out. I was just finishing up sending a text message when I heard this unusual noise and looked up to see a transport truck with cars driving slowly pass us and disappeared past the foliage just ahead of us. It couldn't have been a more exact moment, clearly God's orchestration! As Ladybug and I made our way down an incline driveway, the truck had now turned into a large uncrowded shopping center so the driver could unload the car and maneuver his way out of the space.

The driver had noticed me standing and called me on the phone. *"Is that you?"* He asked and I said, *"yes."* At this time the power of G-d's glory overwhelmed me suddenly, and I began to weep. It was a moment of gratefulness to have a car again. It is so important to take a pause from the many things we are so privileged to have and not to take things for granted! We must be sensitive to what is around us and what is really going on. We must constantly be aware of the smallest of things on a daily basis. He takes us through things to keep us dependent on Him!

We will be seeing so many shifts, and we must be willing to go with the flow. I stood across the street watching the driver take my car off his truck. Most of the deliveries were going to Georgia, his home state, and my car was the first delivery. I felt this was a prophetic statement; this was a new release as the Lord said, *"Now it begins."*

I was so grateful for the things that I had taken for granted. I just wanted to worship G-d for His goodness. This was His love gift to me on Valentine's day.

I felt I need to make others aware of the importance to take time off to really look around and see what G-d wants us to see. Not to measure anything in your current situation, but just pay attention and hear G-d speak. There are so many people needing you and me, but we can be so insular unless we are out of our ordinary surroundings!

Extended Stay America: South Fort Worth, Texas February 21, 2016, Sunday The Last Day In A Hotel

It has gotten colder here, and Ladybug and I are now tucked away behind the hotel that we had just stayed in. We will be sleeping in the car tonight. Strangely enough, at this point, we were unable to contact anyone who would open up a place for us. It is raining, but it feels safe, and between dozing on and off, we have to turn the car on for a little heat now and then. Ladybug is warmly wrapped up in my lap in my very warm sweater coat. I am so happy that I have purchased this very practical garment. We are as safe as we can be considering the circumstances that we are faced with. *"Father protect us and keep us safe."*

Now, back in the hotel, I have completely run out of finances and have no place to go. *"G-d what do we do? You never fail us, there are currently no doors open for us to move."*

Truly, there are many, many people like us in this state tonight but many who are oblivious of these situations. We are generally a prosperous nation and experience teaches us that life has many twists and turns. I had always opened my home to those who needed short-term accommodations and I was never territorial because I wanted people to be comfortable and relaxed while they were there. There is always room for more, especially if you are in a very hard place.

Euless Texas: A Bible Study For A Different Generation, February 23, 2016

I got a message early the next morning from my friend April saying that she was thinking of driving from Branson, Missouri to attend a Bible study outside of Dallas, Texas which was north of where I was. I told her Ladybug and I had slept in my car the night before in the cold and rain and I did not know where I was to go next! We had run out of money! She suggested I call the man who hosted the Bible study to see if I could attend. I would also have to let him know that I had Ladybug with me, and it would be too cold to leave her alone in the car. They kindly agreed for us both to come. I got lost and drove an hour south! GPS is not good here on my phone in Texas. It took me way south to a city with a similar name.

I suddenly realized that I was going in the wrong direction and I would be late for the Bible study. I shouted out, *"Lord, You said You would give me a home of my own with no more moving and rest from all of my enemies and that You would put the solitary in a family!"* I rerouted and headed back to the city of Euless, arriving a little late for the study.

It was very senior group including Pentecostal leaders who reminisced of seasons gone before. The leaders who opened their home had really good hearts and the discussion that night was very different than what I had ever experienced so it was quite interesting to listen and observe. A couple walked into the Bible study late in the evening, very well put together, nice looking couple. They would be angels in the flesh for me and little Ladybug.

There were refreshments and fellowship after the meeting. As people fellowshipped, I was able to speak with the husband and found out he was a doctor, they had also lived in California and attended Pepperdine College in Malibu. They personally invited me to the AIPAC event for Israel being held in at the Performing Arts Center in Dallas in a few days.

I said I would pray about it and would text her later. I had to consider that a lot of my things were in storage and if I have the right attire to attend an event like this? I did pray about it and felt it would be a good thing to attend. I hoped I would have appropriate attire that I could wear in the suitcases in my car.

I decided it would be prudent to stay in the area as my resources were slim and I would not have enough gas to travel back to Fort Worth. This was a wise decision, and since I did not have a place to stay, I would remain in this same area until I knew where to go. So, Ladybug and I would try to make the best of it, pretty much staying warm in the car for the next two days, until we got further instructions!

Bartonville, Texas North Of Dallas February 25, 2016 From The Pit To The Palace

Two days later, as Ladybug and I had just begun to hunker down in the car again for the night, I got a text at about 12:30 a.m. It was from the Doctor's wife. She stated that she might have a friend to assist me regarding a possible place to stay. It was such a relief to see if we could just settle for a few weeks and get things in a better order.

It was at this moment that Ladybug barked to go outside to do her business. I stated this to my friend via text, and she asked where I was. I texted back that I was at a gas station. She again repeated the question, *"Where are you?"* Now, she began to put two and two together as I repeated the same answer. Immediately, she gave the phone to her husband, as she asked him to give me driving directions to their home and the brick guest house on the property. She told me that she would get things set up for me to come to spend the night. In an instant of G-d's mercy, the landscape of my situation would change in that moment. I was grateful beyond measure and a bit alarmed. It was very late, and I was tired and would arrive in the middle of the night.

I'm sure this was interesting for the Doctor to accommodate a stranger at a moment's notice in the middle of the night. But as I got to know my beautiful new friend a bit, she had the biggest spontaneous heart of anyone I had known in a very long time. She was completely free to serve people at a moment's notice and was in a position to do all these things more spontaneously than most.

I was totally shocked by the lack of automobiles on the road in the night season as I drove to this very prestigious neighborhood in North Dallas. So unlike California, people were not out driving on the streets but were all home late at night comfortably tucked into their beds! It felt like I was in a ghost town. Along the roadway, it looked very much like Orange County, with lovely little strip malls, stores and restaurants, many of which had familiar names like those I knew in California.

When I arrived at the address, I was awestruck by the neighborhood. The homes were lovely, each set apart on spacious land between them but no fences. This was a very different landscape for me. It was, of course, a well-manicured, wealthy neighborhood but so casual to California living. I entered the circular driveway and parked as instructed. I texted for instructions, but no answer. I knocked at the door, again no answer. It was now 3:30 a.m., so I walked around the building and saw the guest house. Amazingly, the door was unlocked, so Ladybug and I walked in. It was lovely with a winding metal staircase to a loft above the main floor. There was no bed in the tiny bedroom but a lovely area rug on the hardwood floor in the common area that was more than inviting. We quickly fell asleep on the area rug.

Bright and early, the husband, a medical doctor, with a very large busy practice poked his head around the door. He was about to leave for his office and stated that his wife wanted to see me as they would be on their way for the day. It was a bit hard to be alert but so necessary.

We were still very tired and was greeted warmly with love and taken to a bedroom that was beautifully decorated to honor the country of Israel with beautiful shades of blue representing the country's colours. This was definitely set up for accommodation for the sojourner and this family truly knew how to serve a sojourner.

She was a very energetic woman who moved at a hectic pace. I was invited to rest there through the morning but was given instructions and directions to go to a hair salon and have my hair done later that day. I was overwhelmed with enormous gratitude and the kindness to me, and the hands extended immediately without reservation and expense. It was very humbling. Ladybug and I now settled down to rest and sleep. We were complete strangers but treated so kindly. The next evening our host was out and about with the planning of the upcoming AIPAC event. She asked that I meet her for dinner at a restaurant where she took the time to know who I was. As we left the restaurant, I noticed a Chico's store across the way and casually mentioned that I loved Chico's clothes.

The next evening a bed was brought into the bedroom of the guest house. I was eager to get to sleep, especially after sleeping in the car for a few days and sleeping on the floor the night before. It would be awesome to be in a bed and feel safe and secure.

A bit later, there was a knock on the guest house door and the doctor came in and handed me some money saying, *"we wanted you to go to Chico's and get something to wear to church the next day."* I was stunned; it was overwhelming me at this point. I had never ever been treated so kindly by complete strangers.

Though tired, I went off to Chico's and was treated kindly by a lovely sales lady who helped me get the most discounts for the money I had, and I got some very lovely things to look very presentable for church the next day, as well as for the Jewish celebration. I was blessed with just a bit of money left over to show gratitude and purchase some flowers for my hostess. I joined the family and friends for the Jewish celebration which was focused on honoring and protecting Israel. It was a wonderful event, and I met some beautiful, Jewish dignitaries!

During the weeks I was a guest here in Bartonville, I attended several Jewish fundraisers for Jewish causes, a birthday party in a private home with lovely food for a Holocaust Survivor and a Sunday church service. The family traveled a lot, so were away several weekends.

I was invited to get my things out of storage and set up in the guest house. For all practical purposes, my hostess was allowing me to set up as if I could have enough time in the house to get settled and stay for a bit of time. She was generously going to allow me to store what I could not use, in a storage shed on the property. These were things that I could not put in the guest house. It was a lot to unpack from much damaged boxes that we brought on the property then to repack things in newer boxes to store for later.

My hosts had also purchased a few copies of my original books, Second Edition Prayer Strategy: G-d's Provocative Plan for Wealth and were reviewing them. There was some conversation about me possibly teaching at a Bible study at their office. This would be a real honor and a way to give back and serve their staff.

One morning, there were two brand new suitcases on the porch of the guest house with a note that said that these suitcases were for my travel to Israel. I was floored! Knowing this sojourner assignment would not be short-term, returning to Israel would not be on my radar for a very long time. This would be a season that I have to plead, *"please do not do so much for me!"* Some things she offered I felt from a practical side, I could do myself; like wash my car and clean it out. I know it would not be right to have some things done for me, though her generosity seemed endless in so many ways.

I would come to know more history of this generous family. They are generous to a fault and took or invited me to many social events for the Jewish culture around Dallas. They had received a word from Prophet Kim Clement that they would be supporting Israel and they would prosper from this and surely, without a doubt this was in evidence! The Doctor had been Prophet Kim Clements personal physician during his years living in Texas, and I'm sure he was also the doctor for Kim's large family as well.

They lived three doors from the Prophet John Paul Jackson's widow, who was now selling and moving out of their large home down the street. Roland Baker from Iris Ministries in Mozambique had stayed in this guest cottage. He went through a very difficult illness and had to be sent to Germany for complete restoration for many months, after years of obedience on the African mission field. Other high-ranking Christian guests had stayed here, so it was humbling to stay in the same place as some of these formidable Christian leaders.

This wonderful couple had raised a large family which was still expanding with marriages and grandchildren on the way. How excited and blessed to have such a wonderful family. Even with life's challenges, this was a powerful group who were out to shift cultures on earth as it is in Heaven. They are abundantly blessed as they bless so many along the path demonstrating how to become love on earth. This is truly a pure trading floor. It may not be as spontaneous for everyone to trade into the lives all around them on various levels, but this family was extraordinary in serving the needs of others. It has been an honor to know them and humbled that they were a part of this sojourner's path!

Bartonville, Texas: The Dream Of Preparation For Another Shift On March 11, 2016

I had a dream while staying in the red brick guest house on the property of the wonderful, generous family, that I had just received an inheritance and I started on a journey with some people. I knew at the beginning it would be easy. The journey began inside a building with beautiful hardwood floors. It seemed like in order to start this journey I would be able to glide on the floors that looked like a modern version of the old "fun-house" when I was a kid growing up! We would go up to a high point and we slid down the hill on a gunny sack. It was like a giant slide! This building was very new and modern, but I had to negotiate turns like sharp square corners intersecting a corner of a room! These sharp-angles or square corners would come up from time to time, as I slid down a reasonable way as if going down a hill! It had to be maneuvered really well!

It seemed I would have at least a good month to use the inheritance freely and would share the money with the others so we could all make the trip. I was willing to go for the long haul, but instinctively I knew that it would take a deeper level of faith because the weather ahead would be like winter in a mountain range. And instead of inside on modern floors, we would be outside in the cold weather. When I woke up it was 3:02 a.m.! I knew this was G-d speaking to me.

As I was getting unpacked with all my things from storage and trying to get somewhat settled, I began to engage and set up personal morning prayers to hear the heart of G-d. I knew my assignment was to pray for this family in some very practical areas. Some things were needed, and I was sent there to be involved in prayer and be a catalyst of prayer.

Early one morning my hostess asked me to meet her in the main house to let me know that because of a family emergency, a family member would need a place to stay and so they would need the guest house by the next Tuesday. This was three days after I had received the dream. I felt there was still a lot of spiritual work to do and I had barely begun to understand my assignment. But I also could have gotten too comfortable because of the extreme generosity! G-d had further refining and trust that had to be developed along the way of this sojourner's assignment. This couple truly have a heart to obey G-d and to wholly serve with all that they have.

I was so blessed to have been selected to stay there for the short term I did! I settled in my heart that when I am settled and in my own home again, I would need to reconnect with them. I am finding by being in so many different environments, that G-d does want a lot more time with us; just being with Him and embracing a quiet time to hear and refuel. Although this seems impossible, I see how these very busy and wonderful people are trying to balance this. This seems to be challenging in the lives of these lovely and busy people.

I now had to search for an elusive 5x5 storage space, and they were a rare find. I was returning to my car after looking at one and there on my car window was a ladybug! It seemed G-d was saying everything was going to be alright! One of my host's sons kindly gave some help to move my things to a new storage location. I had a beautiful huge mirror that I sold which provided funds to have Ladybug groomed and for me to purchase a huge, beautiful flower arrangement for my hosts.

G-d's Immediate Miraculous Provision, The Next Location...Mid-Cities Texas: Tuesday March 22, 2016

I was beginning to know the locations, directions and the verbiage about the state of Texas. I was heading sixty miles south of Bartonville where I was staying in North Dallas to Mid-Cities (Texas), to a city called Venus. It was a very rural location with a population of about 3000 people. It is an older town but has always been very small. I was so very mesmerized with the vast amounts of land and open spaces. Endless fields of green grass with a few conspicuously placed large factories in the middle of nowhere! Wow! Texas was a vast area of open space!

I was travelling to this small town in mid-cities Texas because unexpectedly I had received a call from a new friend I had connected with on Facebook. Cheri had just arrived back in Texas and her family would be travelling to Italy and offered me a place to stay until they returned. The trip to Italy would be the trip of a lifetime for this family. Amazing G-d! The door opened for the next part of the journey immediately and I was so grateful!

G-d had impeccably timed it to coincide with my need for a place to stay and miraculously, it had a key amenity, Wi-Fi! I can now focus on writing this incredible journey! G-d's glory and exceptional love never fails. Mercy is new every morning! He graciously engages us to be with the right people of His choice in every situation.

The town square looked neglected and rundown but was flanked on one side by a modern new fire department station and police department. On the other side of the grassy knoll area was about six original buildings which must have been built over sixty years ago. Not all of the businesses in this section where occupied and operational.

In the mix were some beautifully restored Victorians, while others were so dilapidated that they should have been condemned and torn down, but alarmingly they still housed people. It was very strange to see they also had more contemporary homes, and some were new builds. The home I stayed in was a more contemporary home. Behind the property was a cavernous, grassy field that separated the property from a community of modern buildings. There are often no fences in Texas, and it feels like the land goes on forever!

Cheri and I attended some of the local Christian house meetings in the Fort Worth suburbs. We were fortunate to be invited to a private, smaller meeting with a speaker who gave us deep things to ponder. It was refreshing and exhilarating. I was so very moved that I wept through the entire evening.

Passover Dinner

The leaders of the group hosted a beautiful Passover dinner on their farm property. It was a known destination on a very remote country road, very rustic and was used for many events and weddings. They had a huge open barn with the addition of a Bed and Breakfast also built onto the property

Looking back, it was very humorous. It was so remote I got lost. It was an "event" to be lost for an hour and finally get there! I drove all over trying to find it. The street names are actually called County Road with numbers following. This was all new for a former California girl. I pressed on, trying to find the location and when I thought there could not be one more farm there it was; finally, the right location! It was so desolate for a non-native!

Cheri and I was able to spend some time together before she went on her trip. We went to Cracker Barrel, (which was my first time), a popular, southern styled restaurant with a beautiful boutique and restaurant, indigenous to the south and Southern cooking. I also had the chance to go out with her and another lady for breakfast. Gina had come to Texas for a season as well. It was wonderful to be with these amazing, beautiful women just having some fun! Cheri helped me in the developmental stages of the Ladybug Loves cake pops and invested a lot into me when I began to make and prepare these products.

The Dream Of All Dreams

Since my original assignment many years ago was to build prayer around businesses and finances, I began to ask G-d about businesses. I really needed to know His heart at this time about where I was on this journey and what the eternal plan of His original intent is in this. I simply asked Him for a dream. I had never done that before and that night, I had the most magnificent dream! It was mind-blowing!

Here Is The Dream.

I was in New York City and in a large foyer of a huge building with floor to ceiling windows waiting for the elevator with twenty other people. As we waited for the elevator, a beautiful young woman dressed in business attire, a beige coat over a matching dress, came running towards me catty-corner across the foyer. She grabbed my left pants pocket and shoved something in it. Immediately, the elevator doors opened, and we had to rush into the elevator for our appointment upstairs.

Now, this dream, mind you, was in May 2016. And I must insert here that we were approaching the most important Presidential election in my lifetime, but it was way before candidates were announced, running and selected in the fall.

As we got to the floor of our meeting where we had been selected to meet with Donald Trump, it was noted that he was going to pursue the presidency of the USA. We each had been chosen, these twenty people, to meet briefly with the then Mr. Trump, and to speak into his life. What an incredible honor to have been chosen!

When I met with him, of course, I graciously thanked him for the honor of speaking with him. We sat down on chairs across from each other there was no table between us. He leaned in and listened intently to what I was saying, his gaze focused; his lips pursed. I began to speak, and he nodded. I had a brief but powerful message. *"Mr. Trump I'm here to tell you that the most important government that you need to know is the government of the kingdom of heaven under the priesthood of the order of Melchizedek. It is an eternal government, and it is of greatest importance to you."* And this is all that I had to state. As we got up, he shook my hand thanked me, and we walked back to where I handed him off to the next person. Then I went back to wait where I had been with him.

Within a few minutes he came back to me, took my right hand (the right hand is known to mean government), and placed ten thousand dollars cash in my hand and turned and walked away. I was stunned! As I was taking this in, I suddenly remembered that this young woman had placed something in my left pocket, and I had not had time to check it out. I put my hand in my pocket; I was astonished as I pulled out another ten thousand dollars in cash! I woke up with a start and was surprised that I was in a dream. The dream was so real that I just knew it really had happened and I was there! It took my breath away. I knew somewhere in time this was a place and I had traveled there in this dream and it really happened. I was stunned!

I knew there would be the unveiling of this dream in relation to the authority and leadership that is on my life to assist those who have no voice. G-d is serious about the plight of the many but also, touching the one. This powerful dream is now connected to another prophetic voice who has spoken to me about things to come that will be released at the appointed time. Only G-d can orchestrate His glorious plan on such a journey. To say I am undone is an understatement!

My Next Encounter, As I Stayed In Mid-Cities, Was To Begin To Deeply Unravel My True Identity.

When the family left on their trip, I continued to write. With limited finances I could not go too far so Ladybug and I would often go out for walks. We happened to stumble upon some small open market-places; so glad to be out in community from time to time, but the hot Texas climate usually kept us in a good part of the day.

As I continued my studies, I had a very deep experience and encounter that had me weeping for weeks. I received more revelation about my beginning and my true identity. My mother, in dealing with her own torment, had failed to tell me of my Jewish heritage which I would discover in my teens. I had no understanding that one's birth and one's death were very highly esteemed times in the Jewish traditions.

I would learn of the true culture I was formed out of in small increments along the next few years until I could fully embrace the lost power and traditions so necessary to understand one's true identity.

My Personal Experience On The Importance Of Our Biological DNA

On this journey of disenfranchisement, there was a time in my studies of cultural identity that I had to come face to face with the reality of what I was beginning to learn. When mourning the truth revealed my true Identity, I wept for weeks knowing that a significant part of my life was a lie. My mother had meticulously traded on a religious trading floor, the deception of my DNA, which was hidden because of her personal torment of being a divorced Catholic woman who was pregnant by a Jewish man. That would not be popular in her days! I was now realizing that I was not affirmed by my mother because I was her torment being half Jewish and was not able to reconcile this in the time she was alive. She, a devout, religious Catholic had conceived a Jewish daughter out of wedlock. Unthinkable!

In hindsight, the bewilderment of her decision and my discovery in my early teens did not prepare me how to delve for the pertinent information I needed and to ask the right questions to have future options. I had no understanding of how our identity and life's mission is our innate calling embedded in our culture and must be formed properly from birth forward.

My mother did not reveal this truth to me of my rich heritage and instead, in her pain, she tried to make me an extension of herself though we were very different from each other. Now that I am understanding the depth of the Jewish mindset, I am understanding why we were so different. I was drawn to the Jewish traditions so as I am now being trained in the nuances of the culture and the importance of how they live their lives in a direct G-d ordained order! It is a travesty that I had no understanding about how to explore this earlier in my life. Truly, this saddens me now.

But my culture screamed out and looking back I realize that I had so many traits that identified my culture. However, my mother's ignorance of the Jewish culture denied me from knowing my true identity. Though she had told another family member, she passed away without me personally hearing it from her. Through DNA testing eleven years after her death, it was confirmed! I am 48.8%, Ashkenazi Jew.

We had a difficult relationship and now I understand it was based on my mother's fears. However, G-d provided me with a father who was a very good man and a true father to me. I honor him for his kindness to me and for embracing me as his own with love. I asked G-d to reveal to me the hidden and secret mysteries that I did not know. This was the prompting of Holy Spirit to reveal who I was and what was written on my scroll of destiny! It has been a very long journey and is still evolving in this current season that the necessity to know so much more has only begun in the last two years! I have a lifetime to redeem!

I was robbed of the one true rabbinical mystical foundation of my Jewish heritage. I never learned the Torah and I was not taught the Hebrew language of the living letters. I did not have a rite of passage and presentation at Bat Mitzvah and I was never taught that my future companion would come to me from Heaven. Until now, I did not know that there are five steps of engagement and preparation in the Jewish marriage called Ketubah. This in itself should be seriously considered as part of the preparation among young people in American culture. The grave loss of honor of the marriage covenant and its G-d ordained power has been terribly obstructed and defiled!

It should be the central most honored relationship on earth between a man, and a woman as it gives a pure path in courtship. The home is where the heart is, and family is the heart of spirituality, health, wellness, and successes. I did not know the deep spiritual traditions of the Jewish wedding which, when encountered, brings very deep intimacy, spiritually, and through the holiness of the commitment of this marriage ceremony, to build a solid family foundation as the Bible states:

"And the Lord G-d caused a deep sleep to fall upon Adam; and while he slept, He took one of his ribs or a part of his side and closed up the [place with] flesh. And the rib or part of his side which the Lord G-d had taken from the man He built up and made into a woman, and He brought her to the man. Then Adam said, this [creature] is now bone of my bones and flesh of my flesh; she shall be called Woman, because she was taken out of a man. Therefore, a man shall leave his father and his mother and shall become united and cleave to his wife, and they shall become one flesh." (Genesis 2:21-24 AMP)

We simply need to bring this to the attention to the lost youth of this nation! Unfortunately, we seem to have perverted role models today. Torah was and is of G-d, it should never have been stolen from us by Emperor Constantine! In his book, *Lightning from the Master's House, Jason C.N. Jordan* states, *Warning:* Unlike the first book I wrote, this volume is not written for comfortable Christians! It is written for Nazarene Israelites, Jews or individuals who are seriously considering leaving a "church" environment.

Ignored by 99% of religious institutions who profess to follow the Bible is the fact that the Jews were just one of twelve tribes that accepted the whole yoke of the Torah at Mount Sinai. This truth, plainly readable in the most diluted Bible translation, causes the common view of the Old Testament laws being just for Jews, to disappear in a nanosecond. Furthermore, the Bible attests to the Torah's suitability for all mankind.

"One Torah shall be to him that is home-born, and to the stranger

that sojourns among you" (Exodus 12:49).

Ignorance of this fact, has robbed thousands, if not millions, of believers of their core mission directive, to sift Israel from the nations and, like Messiah, only go *"...to the Lost Sheep of the House of Israel."* Rebbe Yahshua, (who most of the world calls "Jesus"), didn't come to save "the lost," but "what was lost." What appears as simple semantics is actually the key to truly understanding the full messianic message of the Scriptures.

This last season, G-d thrusting me out as a sojourner or what is known in Hebrew as *Ger*, is not about to end, as His words that I had to "become the message and see through a different lens," has only brought me to the beginning of my true identity!

Texas June 6, 2016: Nights With No Place to go; 4 Days In The Sweltering Heat Of Irving, Texas

I can't remember a time that G-d allowed so much for us to overcome all at once. It is a time I have never experienced before! I had spent time developing Ladybug Products and had gathered a lot of connections everywhere I went, but I had no permanent location to start a business platform. It was hit and misses as orders came in, but it was not a legitimate business by any means.

My discoveries had been painful and the emotions of being in homes of lovely people were challenging because not only did I have to adapt to their normal, but they also had to adapt to me being in their home changing their normal. It was quite the learning experience because outside of the Jewish life, no one has been taught to truly assist the sojourner among them. The culture of the USA can at times be very insular and that is much of the reason I was sent on this journey. To not only see the diverse, but as a much unplanned experience to bring in others during difficult situations for seasons of time.

There is something called the Jewish mindset which is part of the culture. Jews live to give it and it is powerful. They live to engage with humanity and bring people forward. My whole inner being screams for this. I must be gracious in the generosity that was extended, but my heart hurts to see the plight of the lives of those who have named themselves "Christians." This word was never once used by Jesus. The more I have understood the current seasons in G-d, the more distant I am from the outward forms of "religion." It is a sad state to see people naming the name of Christianity but not having any real deep outflow of a deep spiritual compunction and union with G-d, His plan and His ways!

We need community, like the Jews, who take care of their own and assist the lives of all in their path to come out of difficulty to improve and prosper! Community is the greatest thing missing in America today. We cast out our elderly and youth and those who suffer. It is a disparity that we don't form groups, neighborhoods, and communities to look after our own and those around us. G-d has blessed those who have large or extended families, but the fatherless and the widowed are the single moms of this generation. We have the graying of America as the baby boomers are aging in large numbers. I heard from a registered nurse in Boston, who works with the Veteran's Assistance, that the elderly is being abandoned in their greatest hour of need.

No Interim Place To Stay: Sojourner; Texas June 21, 2016

I rose around 6:30 a.m. in the parking lot in my car in front of 24-hour Fitness. So strange a feeling of where am I! I was really tired when I arrived here last night, and I must have had the air on and fell asleep quickly, because I woke up feeling the humidity. I tried to start the car, and it would not turn over!

I definitely had to shower! It clearly shows how life goes on around us without even considering the plight of those who do not have the convenience of taking a shower. It was not the norm for me to not have the freedom to take a decent shower and it had been two days without the convenience of one and I was very sticky! With my free membership at the 24-hour Fitness, I was able to do so and it sure felt good!

Triple AAA came checked the battery for me later that night. The battery was fine, and the alternator was ok. Thank G-d for that! Whew, two down! The engine light was flashing, so the gentleman told me that AAA has a place the car can be taken to be checked out. Then he finished by saying, *"now you can go home and be safe!"* Wow! Really deep from this perspective … *"go home"* …wistfully I breathed these words! Home? Oops, I had no home to go to. It made me really focus on desiring a home. How long is this journey going to be? I wondered how many others in just this Metro plex area are invisible. How many people here in Irving, Texas were unseen, not being cared for, and enduring the lack of a permanent home?

My Computer Was Stolen, But Angels Pursued It

I was given enough funds to book a night at a hotel. The next day, while shifting out of one hotel into another place that was better at a good, reduced price, I needed my computer and iPhone to work. I had to make the reservation online for the next location. The iPhone battery had died and wouldn't charge in my car. I needed to plug it in at a Starbucks to also use the computer to research the hotel accommodations!

The problem was Ladybug; she could not stay in the car because of the sweltering heat! As I went into Starbucks, using the Wi-Fi was a problem as dogs were not allowed inside. So, the manager took me outside to see if there were any plugs on the building walls. I simply laid my computer on a table just inside the door as we were feet away and we opened the side door!

A woman quickly walked past me as we re-entered the store with the manager. She simply said to me as she walked past, *"thank you."* I thought, rather polite but kind of odd. My next experience was about to jolt me as I went back into Starbucks, my computer was gone! This polite comment from the woman who was passing me was because she had stolen my computer! Of course, it flashed on me that this computer had all of my writings and books, etc.! It was a moment in time I had to instantly rest on G-d! I called my dearest friend Bill in

California to solicit his counseling help, and he said, *"Ask to see the cameras film in the store and make a police report."* I did both, *and* now I would have to just patiently wait. I had to trust G-d and stay in a state of peace and rest and could do nothing except make the reservations for the next hotel on the phone and go to my next location, one with a complete kitchen.

I called all my strong praying friends and asked them to go into the courts of Heaven and pray on my behalf to get my computer back. I do believe in the power of prayer and engaging the angelic to bring back the computer for me is scriptural because they work on our behalf. I forgave the woman who stole it. I was grateful it was on lockout, so she would have to be swift to know how to break into it. I stayed in faith and focused as G-d knew that all my writings, including this book, were in that computer. Who knew if anything was backed up because of my unusual existence these past few months? I got the call from the police about my report, and then I got a call from Starbucks to come and get the computer because someone had brought it back.

It was exciting to see the hand of G-d and angelic intervention because it was returned four days later to the Starbucks it was stolen from. The woman just returned it by dropping it off. The team that wrote it all up was not working that day, so they did not know all of the stories. I called the police and could have pursued charges and an arrest, but I chose to forgive this person and move on. My prayer for her is she never again steals someone's computer and would be convicted of any further desire to steal things. G-d was supernaturally faithful! But the most daunting part now is, I really do not have a residence, and it is not safe.

After these last few days, following this dramatic situation, I had exhausted the non-existent places to seek help from, and there was no immediate place to stay again; *"Father G-d I need your help."* All of this clearly showed me why G-d allowed these last eight months walking in this path! I was learning daily the "whys" of what He has put in me. Also, understanding the very great need to help with practical short-term needs for single women and children and now, learning about the new disenfranchised, displaced functioning seniors. It will be to show and bring them to the greatest level of successes, by first rebuilding the kingdom within them.

I had to experience firsthand—what it was like staying and sleeping in my car for two days and nights in the sweltering Texas heat! We simply do not perceive all that goes on in our own world of comfort ... it is always just invisible from our lifestyles! We don't see the need when there is little engagement.

Putting Your Mother On The Street!

I came across a story of a lovely senior woman in Australia who lived in the home she owned with her husband. When he died, her two daughters took over the home and moved in with her with at least one grandchild. It seemed to be a good mix of the generations all in one common place assisting each other. Then at a certain time, the daughters told their mother it was their house now and that she needed to leave. Again, how can this be? How can adult children be so callous and not consider an aging parent? They gave her a date, let her sleep on a sun porch and at their appointed time, took her with a suitcase and dropped her off on a downtown street. It's hard to hear a story like this, but clearly there has been a shift in the honoring of the aging in societies.

"Honor widows who are truly widows. But if a widow has children or grandchildren, let them first learn to show G-dliness to their own household and to make some return to their parents, for this is pleasing in the sight of G-d." (1 Timothy 5:3-4 ESV)

June 20, 2016

As I was driving south, my car started to shake, and the engine light went off. Not good!

Today, it's Father's Day celebrations for everyone but we only have the heavenly Father who is the ultimate Father.

Well, we are now without accommodations again as we ran out of all of our money. This was our first night to sleep in the car for a long time, and IT IS A HOT TEXAS SUMMER!

Texas Unbearable Heat June 23, 2016, Irving

I now sat outside of Starbucks in a beautiful setting in Irving, Texas. It was a similar community much like Orange County — very contemporary and prosperous. My thoughts were on the difficulty at hand, to be able to get a place to live.

The heat was ghastly but if I sat outside of Starbucks, I could get Wi-Fi and Ladybug could sit on my lap. We could do this while our car was parked in the shade to stay cooler and also to take a bit of time in the car putting the air on for a cool breeze to soften the relentless Texas heat.

A lovely Jewish businesswoman, sitting at the table next to me, and I were having a conversation while she waited for a client. She could not see Ladybug behind my computer screen so was quite surprised to hear a dog bark. She was a business coach for women in sales and had her own radio show. We had a delightful conversation. It was quite uplifting as I began to tell her my story. She made some great suggestions, but those would have to play out when I get settled in a permanent location. Hopefully we will meet again along the way.

How Does One Get Into A Home?

The waiting list which I contacted for an affordable or subsidized housing is a very long, eighteen months process in this part of Texas. A process which is very impractical for people with immediate needs. I pondered on how many seniors are in this same place today with no one, no faith, no compassionate family to help them? It is unconscionable not to assist families or friends in these real situations!

The reality is more intense when you need basic identifying things to be connected legally in the American way of life. To apply for a driver's license or transfer your residence from state to state varies.

You may need your birth certificate to apply. You must be able to confirm your current legal address. You also may require a utility bill to show that you pay these bills from this address. You cannot rent a P.O. Box unless you have a current address where you reside, and you can't get car insurance or register your car as well. You cannot renew your passport either or get a passport. These are very basic things that we take for granted daily. It is a very slippery slope. I have found on this road less traveled, that in China, it is against the law to not take care of your parents after 60 years of age!

Although, I know that ultimately, it was only G-d who was going to provide for me at this point, I tried to establish a Go-Fund me page to let people know that I needed some assistance in starting sustainability. I was weary of this condition but felt it might pick up some compassion from the business community. As upbeat as I made it, no one responded to consider working with me to build the project that I had tried to establish through this season: I don't think there was a sensitivity to read the underlying factors. The simplicity of what needs to be established to get focused, especially because I had always been very successful in business in the past.

Through the compassion of a kind friend in another state, I was connected with some local people who allowed me and Ladybug to have provisions at Red Roof Inn hotel in Plano, Texas for two days. It was a welcomed reprieve from the scorching heat and not having to sleep in the car! It gave us the time to use resources to get the car cleaned well, get a few bills paid and do some laundry. We truly rested well and met some more incredible people.

Ladybug was able to get a good shower in the morning and ate a good breakfast. We got salads the day before at the Trader Joes across from the carwash as well as a new bag of her important dog food. She is resilient like me, and we are doing well. I am thanking Father for His heart for those who have no choices. It is breaking my heart about the unseen people, who are my age and have no one! Weeping for them this morning! To even qualify for off-market rates for affordable housing in this state like so many, is a huge wait. Where do these people go?

When I left Bartonville (North Dallas) at the end of March, I had a dream, and in part, it said there would be a bit harder time ahead. I clearly did not want this, but it has to be experiential to feel the infirmities of the suffering and disenfranchised. Even in rest it has been grueling! So, after staying in the parking lot at Motel 6 tonight (where I felt it was safe), we would not be conspicuous as so many are travelers and have loaded cars coming and going all day and night. It was so hot from time to time and even at night I had to wake up and run the air a bit. I am learning new parts of what Texas living is like; very hot summers as predicted. As long as there is a breeze it can be OK but without it, the heat hangs heavy in the air! Need breezes!

Back To Irving Texas

After six days of being in the heat several things happened. I got two large orders of cake pops which would bring in revenue and my friends heard that I was once again living in my car and booked me a hotel for one week in mid cities to be out of the heat. This was my miracle. I had about $400.00 of revenue to earn, and I could now have a kitchen to work in. In addition, there was more money put into my account so that I could purchase products. Thank you, G-d for impeccable timing!

July, Austin, Texas: My Daughter Called Me

A difficult time was ahead. The difficulties of displacement is to walk through what is not a routine to those of another household, including your own child. My daughter and I are polar opposites and so it become difficult when we cannot agree and especially at the times when she seems to forget that I am the mother. She was facing some difficulties and her pain, and her emotions were at times overwhelming for her. The timing impacted what I was doing to move forward on the Ladybug Loves Project.

She contacted me and asked me to come south to Austin and it was really good to see her. She needed a surgery, and I was able to be there for her. At this time, she was already on disability from an accident at the gym. She had a home office and was working on many projects. She was very busy and had a lot going on which clouded our time together.

Austin, Texas: August 2016

The weather has been cooler and this morning I took Ladybug for a walk knowing that we would *"svitz"* profusely as this time of the day. She hates staying inside but sometimes the heat is unbearable! I have been praying on these walks, asking G-d to release what is on my scroll to connect with the people here, learn how to help the people in this area and "network" G-d's plan for Ladybug Loves.

We walked around the newly developed millennials high rise apartments and condo areas as well as specialty stores. As we headed back to my car, we passed the loading zone area in the back of Traders Joes, which seemed to be a loading area, I noticed two cars and a lady wearing a T-shirt on saying: *"Feed Austin!"* and subtitled, *"healthy food!"*

Wow! This warmed my heart and excited me. Austin is an area that has suited up for this situation. It is one of the cities that has taken a huge path to help people who simply needed help. Once I came back in from our walk, I immediately looked up their website!

It Was His Twenty-Third Birthday

I parked in a short-term parking space to go in quickly to do an errand for my daughter, and I noticed a very thin young man, pacing back and forth near the stores in front of me. He had on a dirty shirt indicating he might be homeless. He otherwise looked respectable but in great need. So, I said, *"Lord, what do you want me to do?"* I struggled to get out of the car with Ladybug in tow and as I was putting money in the parking meter he disappeared from my view. I said, *"G-d track him back near me, I don't want to lose him in the crowd! If I'm supposed to talk to him, bring him back."*

I had barely finished my thought when I saw that he had turned around and was walking back to where I was. I called to him and asked him if he had breakfast yet. He said *"no, but it's my birthday."* So, I wished him a happy birthday. His name was Isaac, and he was here from Oklahoma and he had fallen on some hard times. I asked where he wanted to go for breakfast.

As we walked to where he suggested, we engaged in conversation. I bought his breakfast and waited for him outside with Ladybug. He brought his breakfast outside to where we were, and we continued talking. He talked about his grandparents who passed away. They meant a lot to him seemed to have been his grounding. I encouraged him and prayed for him. I then gave him the money I had in my wallet. I don't know if I will ever see him again, but I told him that G-d heard his heart and that is why I approached him to bless him. God wanted to bless him as a father would on a son's birthday! This was all by 8:30 this morning. There is a very ripe harvest out here and Isaac was the one that G-d wanted to touch deeply today through me with some form of provision on his birthday!

Homelessness For Students In Austin, Texas

During my stay in Austin in 2016, I researched how that city was managing homelessness. Can you imagine students being homeless going to school every day? This is real in our nation today. Here are statics that I found in Austin, Texas. The number of homeless students enrolled in Austin Independent School District decreased from 2,693 during the 2015-2016 school years, to 2,311 during the 2016-2017 school years. The number of homeless students was higher during the 2015-2016 school years because of flooding in the Austin area during October of 2015. I can't imagine the difficulty and impact on young lives!

Homeless Plaque In Park In Austin, Texas

On this journey of the sojourner, I continued to stumble upon many elements to draw attention to the plight of the disenfranchised people. Here I was now in Austin, Texas in a hot summer of 2016. I would walk Ladybug and my daughter's dog in the park along the Ladybird

Lake before it became too hot in the day. The lake separated the downtown area, with high rises being built, and the park on the south side.

In the park there is a memorial tree and under the tree is a plaque adorned with little wooden dolls. Each doll represents a human life that has died homeless on the streets of Austin Texas! Sad, tragic, shocking and unthinkable!

The plaque reads: Homelessness:

"It is the essence of depression. It is immoral, it is socially corrupt. And it is an act of violence. In memory to those who have lost their lives in the streets of Austin. House the Homeless, Inc. 1993"

I found this excerpt that read, *"this year we will read the names of over 100 citizens of Austin who died in poverty from October 2016-October 2017."*

"For 24 years, we have gathered on Auditorium Shores, recently re-named Vic Mathias Shores, when we say goodbye to the women, men, and children who have lived and died on our streets in poverty the previous past year. This one-hour service begins at Sunrise which should be at 6:57 a.m." This reference is on the plaque on a tree in the park at First Street and Riverside Drive in Austin, Texas near Ladybird Lake across the lake from downtown Austin. Can you imagine this demise represents a human life that has died homeless on the streets of Austin Texas! And we can't grasp it.

The Dog Groomers In Austin, Texas

My next stop was to take Ladybug to get groomed. In my enthusiasm, I told the grooming salon owner and the groomer Ladybug's story and brought them some Ladybug Love cake-pops for them to enjoy. I asked them where I should go to network her story and products and was given two names. One is an event called Snout to Snout by a Jewish community and the other is "Dog-tober-fest," Austin! This one has 10K attendees! I was getting connections in the area, thank you

G-d.

My dear friend Bill from California had texted me to say he was battling with cancer and asked me to pray for him. He also told me he was building a business that could coincide with the Ladybug Loves Project. I had told him about the two events I had learned about and He and his associate who lived in Dallas, wanted to make plans to help me with attending these events. It seemed we could really do some amazing things to build this entity. It would be a great team effort.

It was very difficult to know Bill was now fighting cancer. He is an incredible man and a treasure to know, and kindness and helpfulness is his mantle. I wanted to stand in prayer for his miracle and also engage with him in his business pursuits. What a dichotomy! Such a lovely man! So kind and funny, generous to a fault! (At this writing, I must sadly say this dearest of people in my life graduated to Heaven October 3, 2017. Heaven is richer; we are sadder, but we know he is in eternity as that is what G-d put in his heart!)

Bill's product was a health and wellness product, both for humans and pets. It would be a real tool and be able to bless people and animals as well, and to support the Ladybug Loves Project! I'm learning how many people love their animals and take such good care of them. After all, our little fur babies are such a delight to us. I did not know I would be leaving Austin before these events. It would have been a great opportunity to form the needed team that I longed for to bring Ladybug Loves Project forward. It would have been wonderful to work with Bill.

My Birthday - August 18, 2016

The date was August 18, 2016, and my daughter kindly took me out for a nice lunch in downtown Austin. I don't remember the location but no matter how high end the restaurants are in Austin, I looked forward to not sitting at a table on a dirt floor. Sure enough, there were slabs of concrete but still a lot of dirt around the tables and chairs where we sat outside to eat.

The weather in Austin can change in an instant! We drove over to Ladybird Lake, passing by where there is a stretch of park and walking area along the river. A few people caught my eye, in particular a man in a yellow sweat suit who appeared to be homeless getting completely drenched in the downpour. Compassion shot straight through me. My immediate reaction was to go to the Goodwill store and purchase him something dry to put on.

After the celebration, I didn't see him on the street that I had seen him earlier. I did go to the Goodwill store (a place throughout the USA to purchase a lot of great second-hand merchandise) and purchased two brand new sweatshirts that still had the tags on them. I went on an elusive journey looking for him but wasn't able to find him. As I was driving around, I saw another homeless man and immediately opened my car window and handed him the sweatshirts. It was not all lost! It is just so hard to see the sea of needy human lives without the basic necessities. I was constantly moved and so sensitive to these things I was taking in.

"For there will never cease to be the needy in your land. Which is why I command you; open your hand to the poor and needy kinsman in your land." (Deuteronomy 15:11)

I couldn't help but resonate on the content of this verse—ever so true.

About To Leave Austin

I would be leaving Austin in a few more days and was looking forward to a much-needed break from all the clamor and activities. A place of rest is so needed to begin to absorb health and wellness. I thank G-d for a home of my own so that I won't have to move anymore and rest from all of my enemies … *"soon, please Lord, hear my petition."*

Miracles Constantly: The End Of September

I had two fender benders and both in parking lots, one of which I needed to get the car repaired. Early one morning I drove about an hour north to the auto repair facility in Georgetown where I had gotten my car inspected repaired before.

This was the second minor accident in one month and I had no idea how I would be able to pay the deductible. Unfortunately, my deductible had doubled with my current insurance company since I left California, going from $250.00 to $500.00 and I simply did not have the necessary funds.

Fortunately for me, this brilliant company had a great marketing department and had posted a sign at the stoplights at the intersection to a freeway entrance. This sign "jumped" out at me and it took a minute to register what it was saying. This company would waive the deductible on all vehicles needing repair! I had never heard of this before, but it was just what I needed right now! Considering it is a new location and the difficult thing is, so many people are going through now, it couldn't be a better win-win solution to bring in new business!

Good-bye Austin

My friend in Palm Beach, Florida invited me to come and spend some time with her. Leaving my daughter at this time was bittersweet. Her path is challenging. My stay had allowed me to discover areas of learning common to the senior community.

The last weeks I was there she had bought the home she desired. All the work involved in assisting her warranted a break from the chaos and much needed rest.

Leaving Austin: October 12, 2016, Arriving In Palm Beach, Florida

I arrived in Palm Beach utterly exhausted and was greeted by my friend who graciously brought me here from Texas. Her compassion was such a relief. I was taken to lunch with her friend, but I was so tired; I just needed rest. I really wasn't very hungry at all. Peace was what I needed. A long-term dear friend of hers provided a place for me to stay temporarily. It was quite refreshing and so needed. Except for taking Ladybug for her walk and to get an occasional coffee, I spent the next three days sleeping: so grateful for peace and quiet.

A Young Homeless Man Waiting For Starbucks To Open

The next morning after my arrival, I woke up early as usual and took Ladybug for a little stroll. I also needed a coffee at the Starbucks in the little shopping center around the corner. It was still quite desolate, as the coffee shop had not opened yet. I heard a voice greeting Ladybug warmly, and I was quite surprised to see someone already there sitting on one of the lounges. He was a gaunt looking young man, so we sat down and talked with him.

He was homeless and I sat and listened as he told me his story. His girlfriend had left him, and he had also lost his residence. He was having trouble holding it all together and then lost his job. He was trying to get back to the state up north where his father lived. We chatted for quite a while. I bought us both a coffee when the store opened and asked him if I could pray with him. I told him I would bring him $20.00 as soon as I could get to an ATM.

It was yet another time that there was a divine engagement for a very short time with another young life. I would have loved to have assisted him further. But all was not lost, as I was given the name of a place in this area that could assist him to get on his feet. This is what happens when we stop for just the one, he told me that he was staying in an abandoned house close by. I emailed him the name of this ministry given to me, and I prayed he would find some assistance through this housing for young men. It sounded spectacular. I wrote about my encounter on my Facebook page and was also given a bit of money to give to him the next time I connected with him.

West Palm Beach is a very charming city, and it was very easy to move around without a vehicle. The proximity to shopping and local transportation made it an excellent resting place.

I walked along the palm tree laden area daily with little ladybug. Being only 5lbs and champaign color, people constantly stopped to talk about how cute she was. I would always tell them about her project, and many wanted to know if we already had a brick-and-mortar store or wanted to jump on board to help. Two couples in particular stood out; a young couple from Abu Dabi who had a lot of family in Palm Beach, and a lot of children in the family who would love her treats. They wanted to know if we had a brick-and-mortar store. Loved that they asked! Another was a young couple who took it upon themselves to begin to design a new logo for us. A very amazing place full of opportunity, but alas, one I would be moving on from very soon.

I was warmly welcomed by some lovely people, friends of my hostess. In her enthusiasm, she had promoted that we would make a large amount of Ladybug Loves products to assist me in my introduction to the area. I loved her enthusiasm, but it would take some planning to set up. Most importantly, I would need a kitchen and would need my baking utensils shipped so I could make the products with limited amount of money. Florida was very cottage food friendly. I had done my homework.

What Do We Do Now?

In hindsight, this group of female leaders were very busy people doing life with many responsibilities. They were really overbooked as one can understand. They were very compassionate, but no one was able to assist or engage in my business/vision as this time. It would take some time and planning to be crafted. I was not positioned in the same spiritual or social lane and it was clear that I was in a different season with varying needs with didn't fit into their current lifestyles.

Their lives were very socially active. They moved very quickly, was quite booked and busy. There was no sign of quiet time. They had a great sisterhood which was very warming, and we all need this but contrary to a previous visit here many years ago, this was a different time. Things had shifted immensely from that time to now. Especially this particular season when I was called to the walk of the sojourner. I would have to walk this out until the end. With each point of understanding releases would come that would eventually end the journey.

I was asked to share on a Monday what I had been learning on my journey. I planned to share a little message about the things that I was learning from a new perspective. I was eager to speak to this casual small group meeting. The sound and the message delved into a much different perspective than which I was invited to speak on and there was a measure of opposition from my hostess, but there was encouraged hunger from the attendees, for the most part. Because of my extreme fatigue travelling to West Palm Beach, I had been pondering on what I should share. I feel it would provoke a desire to learn more, but not all were in agreement.

Sudden Death

One Sunday, shortly after I had arrived, while praying, I heard the words *"sudden death,"* and I pondered on the area that I have currently been temporarily relocated to. What might that mean, or who might that be? Late that evening, I got a call that there had been a "sudden death" of a very prominent woman who had been profoundly successful in business and finances on the east coast. She was part of the women's group that I had just spoken with and she had died suddenly, that very afternoon! There was this uneasy knowing that the week before while in another state, her life had been threatened. There was a premature "spirit of death" surrounding her. Though a formidable woman in business, socially and philanthropically, she had suffered under a cloud of oppression throughout her life.

Needless to say, this has been very disarming and a lot of grief for those who are closely related to this dear woman. I did not sleep much that night but did a lot of research on her, learning more of who she was and about her husband and business partner. She had many "earthly" talents and connections! So talented and seeming such a premature departure! She was highly respected and gave generously into her community in several states. I especially prayed for her husband who said she was *"his world!"*

It was so shocking yet there was still a great need for much compassion for this delicate type of tragedy! I had yet to meet her personally! I was so looking forward to doing so. Now, it will never happen on earth. She probably would have come to the long Monday meeting that I have attended for the last three weeks. These are all very prominent women in this area; some very hungry in this growing group! They have a beautiful sisterhood to be admired! However, there was a light!

The people I am meeting here are just coming into the understanding of the spiritual government teaching, DNA realignment and the engaging of the courtrooms of the kingdom of Heaven. This is still very foreign for them to fully grasp and for them to encounter.

I met an amazing couple here that I call the "fire starters" because of their deep love and desire for so much more! They have traded deeply into the heavenly realms as well. Their son had lost his battle with cancer last year and letting G-d heal their broken hearts with much wisdom. Though they could operate out of their pain, they are the embodiment of love!

Video Church

Attending a "church" here was a totally strange encounter for me since I have been out of religious structures for so long. It is always intriguing to understand the intrinsic value in going to massive places and to see a public display of entertainment devoid of deep, deep intimate adoration and connection with G-d. Is it not an encounter through worship that ushers in an atmosphere and a shift of frequencies of holiness and communion? Their meetings are what is called "campuses" in different locations with video "church." I've long left behind these types of gatherings and meetings. It is often so challenging to go where there is no real engagement with G-d.

I lean more towards small, intimate business to business or house to house groups, who build relationally and intimately. These often bring alignment to the atmosphere of a person's current needs, far exceeding these types of events. There is no compunction to engage in a video church. It's not one of inspiration or a demonstration of changing the neighborhood, the city block, the workplace or the people on our daily path. There are people in our daily circles who are in need of so much love, healing and our network of assistance. This is my heart's cry!

"Father, may your kingdom come, may your will be done on earth as it is in heaven, in Palm Beach County, FL."

Another Shift

It is two days before Thanksgiving, and I am in a motel waiting for a temporary place to stay before making my way back to Texas to get my car.

Yesterday was quite the day! God allowed me to experience the things one would painfully walk through when we don't communicate in love. There were things happening behind the scene that I was not aware of and there seemed to be no end game to this oddity. The ladies were focused on preparing for the Thanksgiving holiday. Now that I am understanding more about the Hebraic foundations through revelation, the "holidays" is one more thing that I have stepped away from. I am now celebrating the Feasts!

I went to the meeting and walked into a very confusing and emotionally painful situation. To my utter dismay, there had been an extensive discussion about the difficult situation I was facing without the consideration of engaging me personally. Of course, not unexpectedly, some things were very much distorted. Judgments were made, accusations were made and needless to say I felt so weighted down dealing with this from such a spiritually mixed group of prosperous and successful female leaders. My friend had been so kind to bring me here from Texas, but it became very challenging for me to understand the cultural and spiritual shifts I was witnessing.

One thing remains sure; G-d is faithful. I am learning so much. We are in a cultural shift that needs perspective, and we have to become love in all circumstances. Assumptions, confrontation and being critical in your conversation without personal engagement is not love. Engaging the spirit of wisdom is the principal thing and in all your getting, get understanding. Move in what you profess in how you express and communicate counsel. We must have a way of conveying what is edifying. When this is mixed with sound advice it will improve and provide measures that will help to rebuild out of the ashes. In extending a hand, and seeking an end game, there should be preparation made as an alternative for the sojourner. *Love the sojourner.*

"Do not neglect to do good and to share what you have, for such sacrifices are pleasing to G-d." (Hebrews 13:16 ESV)

The religious do not understand spiritual shifts and will be resistant preferring to stay with the old ways. It is so difficult to observe the lack of understanding of what is being presented today to expand our knowledge in a world of such transition and crises. We have the opportunity to discern the shift toward Heaven through genuine humility.

"Thank you, Father, for ordering the steps that are of You. I ask for mercy, provision and 2 Samuel 7:10-11, and Your economy, which is the only way. Your provision shall be seen! I am humbling myself, thanking G-d for the next step. My life is in You."

There is a level that G-d is exposing of the things inside of us He wants to change! I am learning that neither religion nor comfort are options. It is humanly impossible to be vulnerable and yet unable to express one's desire to move above the circumstances.

*Blessed are those when men persecute you, revile you and speak all manner against you unjustly for great is your reward in heaven. "For it is not (intended) that other people be eased and relieved (of their responsibility) and you burdened suffer (unfairly), But to the equality (share and share alike), your surplus over necessity at the present time, going to meet their want and to equalize the difference created by it so that at (some other time) their surplus in turn may begin to supply your want. Thus, there may be equality. As it is written, He who gathered much had nothing **over, and he that gathered little had no lack.**"* (2 Corinthians 8.13-15 AMP)

Florida, December 17, 2016: The Haitian Culture

I was faced with the challenge of being in between. I had worked hard at getting the Ladybug Loves Project to the place where it would provide sustainability. The products had been developed and Ladybug Loves project was now set up as a non-profit (done pro bono by my lawyer in California), along with all the by-laws! Now, I was desperately waiting to see how I could leave Florida and get back to Texas so I could get my car operational again. I had to be able to move to the next location of G-d's provision.

But we were now stuck for the moment by the inability to produce income and a place to live. I was in limbo, needing G-d's miracle for this season!

G-d's Humble Angel

My first week in Palm Beach I was invited to attend a Jewish service. It was there that I met Pastor Charles, the most exciting and the most genuine leader in Palm Beach and Brower County, Florida. He immediately understood me and understood the spiritual journey I was on as a sojourner.

Without reservation, he pulled out his wallet as I protested, and immediately gave me funds. Now, in this dilemma I was facing, he would be my "go to person" and would be the catalyst to expedite my last two weeks of housing, safety, and preparations to leave Florida. He is a rare man who serves his community and all those around him, with a loving heart like no one I have seen. He is the epitome of a man who knows that his life is to take care of the fatherless, the widow, the orphan and the sojourner among us. He truly is a living sacrifice.

For the remaining two weeks that would need to stay in the Florida area, Pastor Charles assisted me in finding a place to stay. He connected with a lady he knew, and she was gracious enough to allow me to stay at her place. I was enormously grateful for this door that was opened for me at this brief time.

With such a short time remaining in Florida, I would not be able to sell some of the desserts I had prepared and there was no place to see them. I had to give them away. Pastor Charles was one of the recipients and commented on the excellence of the taste of the gift but also the quality and presentation. It was very encouraging.

When I enter into a new environment, I am usually able to see things with a different lens though sometimes it is hard to get the pulse of the places I am staying. And while grateful, often, there is a test. It is a test for me to remain humble and appreciative and a test to challenge the condition of hearts. Previous places I had stayed had been very challenging. All had their lessons and observations of how the Father wants to shift our cultures and our limited mindsets and this was not any different. Even though religion is a huge lingering factor in most situations, we have moved through different dimensions and ages. We embrace that which Abba is giving us on our scroll of destiny if we are in tune with the current things presented to us. We must embrace the situations at hand.

My host and I were at opposite ends of the personality spectrum and this, I suspect, may be the reason why Pastor Charles had been somewhat hesitant in connecting me with her even though he felt it would be a good transitional place for me until I was able to return to Texas. She had been a profound leader in the North East and a woman of intense prayer, but it seemed that some experiences in life had caused her to become more cautious. I knew she would have preferred that I functioned in this manner, but it was obviously not my style; I am very outgoing.

During the last two weeks in Florida, I knew I would be waiting on G-d to know what the next move would be. A wonderful friend I knew from a speaking engagement many years ago and who also lived in Florida called and offered to pay for the cost of repairing of my car in Texas. *Thank you, G-d for true kindnesses!*

A friend of mine who I knew many years ago had become aware of my situation through her daughter and reached out to me. She and her husband had attended the same Bible school I did over twenty years ago. Miraculously she offered to pay my way back to Texas and even when to the extent of offering to pick me up at Houston airport and drive me to my car in Austin, two hours north of Houston. I was flooded with gratefulness.

If this all came together, I would have some time living with them until I could get started with my business. Unfortunately, there was a clause in their lease that would not allow them to have little Ladybug. It would have been another welcome, very peaceful, and an ideal place of rest. What a gracious family! What love in my friend's heart as she knew me in this different season! My heart was flooded with the generosity of the "body being the body" and receiving a sojourner. It was hard at times not being in one place long enough to set down roots for sustainability.

The next welcomed miracle which came from her was that she deposited $500.00 into my checking account and then an additional $1,000.00! I was undone and beyond grateful! Such joy arose out of these few dark weeks! The kindness of G-d was overwhelming! I was able to book a flight for me and Ladybug with all our expenses taken care of and send the funds to repair the car. Now to get our luggage and things back to Texas. I could now be at ease and overwhelmed with the kindness of G-d.

Being Informed And Educated

Spiritual understanding has been shifting for the last two decades. We cannot operate out of an old culture. People are being developed to move into models that will be consistent with the shakings going on culturally, politically, generationally and worldwide. Former formats cannot contain what we must hunger for in a world that today, looks nothing like twenty years ago.

We are being reintroduced to the spiritual development of the Hebrew culture in the early church which shifted the followers of Yeshua. Why don't people see the sojourner among them? It is important to understand the length of time that would be devoted to getting the sojourner back on track. This is the grace G-d gave to the

Jews, His hand extended; and what an opportunity it is!

When Constantine Made Religion And Institutionalized It

The Church shifted during the time of establishing the Nicene Council led in 325 A.D by the evil intent of Emperor Constantine. It was he who structured an institution, a "church of the state." The violence exploded to dismantle all that had been established of the Hebrew foundations following after Yeshua, and enforced the Constantine model, a structured institution of religion.

In the last twenty years, there has been a mass exodus leaving these archaic institutions. In some cases, it is because they no longer satisfy the longing for the deeper things that were demonstrated throughout first 300 years after Yeshua. Some "Christian churches" are often building outward kingdoms while the Jews helped to build humanity and were taught since birth to be the hand of G-d extended! This is called the Jewish mindset. The depraved condition of the "sheeple" with no real compassion goes to a whole new level. And now, I have experienced it in human form.

On this journey, I have seen a very mixed bag of cultural, religious practices and deceptions under the guise of religion but what is really a much diluted "Christianity." The poor demonstration is an abomination of the true pattern of "Christ." And it cuts to the core of the unsanctified, hardened, hurting and untrained heart of broken people.

People who think that years of religious "training" and degrees are a pedigree and can establish one as a leader is more than scary. Yeshua was of no reputation. His demonstration was only to do what His father said to do. My mentor had this insight: *"We don't decrease so that He can increase; we disappear altogether."* This is how we are being separated, our soul from our spirit. Through death to our fleshly desires, pain, and suffering, our characters are forged in the fires of affliction. And many baptisms of fire will burn away our old way of thinking and our old way of doing things.

The last couple of weeks staying with Marie was difficult. I was in a place of constraint and imposed control because she had one and only one way of operation. Until I was able to leave, it was feeling almost cultish and I was anxious for the awaited "release from captivity" so I could have my personal freedom restored. Fortunately, I was able to go to a hotel for the two remaining days and had some time to rest before my flight back to Texas.

The day I was to move to the hotel, I called Marie at 3:00 p.m. to let her know that I would be coming by to pick up my things. I waited for four hours in the cold night for her to arrive to allow me to pick up my things. It took a long time to get a cab that late in the evening to return to the hotel. I was so grateful to arrive at a place of rest in a hotel to be in peace again.

Seeing the corruption on social conditions was alarming to me. This is not the true ecclesia that Yeshua built. He called us to be humble, caring and to understand what it is to be available as a hand extended with compassion building one another up in love. The sojourner understands that parts of the journey can be very rough.

"Lord, I grieve for Your true ecclesia to come on the scene. Father teach them to become love for the heart that You desire to display."

I tried to extend wisdom on my entrance here, but a culture of darkness was at hand. It is an untrained, unbridled mind, steeped in an old poverty in mindsets, spirits and in the reality of the daily practices.

December 19, 2016: Preparing To Leave Florida

Precious little Ladybug had a recheck at the vet for her ear infection. We had a very good vet this time at Paws2Pay in West Palm Beach. She took a real interest in Ladybug's ear health, correctly training me on how to properly clean Ladybug's ear and information about her meds. Ugh! Now, she is good to go to get on the plane tomorrow morning.

Our last night in Florida was spent at a TYJ hotel overnight near the Fort Lauderdale airport. When we land in Texas, I will be able to pick up my car. It will be so good to have my own transportation again. Thank G-d all the repairs needed are already done.

December 20, 2016: The Day Has Arrived "Yea, G-d, I so need the shift!"

Ladybug and I arrived at my Desi's home in Austin, Texas via a cab costing $38.00! She wasn't home and not being able to find the spare key in the spot where it was supposed to be, it was a bit disconcerting asking the cab driver to leave everything on the curb. So, I called Gary, the gentleman working on my car. Good news! He had needed to purchase a sensor to finish up all the repairs and was on his way to drop off the car. Whew, ok! We would soon have our own wheels! I unloaded the luggage, so we can now begin the rearranging and transfer of the luggage to my car!

Gary is another amazing man, and I am so grateful! Only G-d could have connected us! He had the best price for the repairs needed on my car, ($150.00 less than the commercial business). It is always good to check to see the going rates and compare prices! I found him on the internet and made the arrangements and payments online while I was in Florida. He did the repairs onsite which saved me money and time and his work was of the highest quality. It couldn't get any better!

Gary's kindness extended to me was beyond what I could have expected. There was an additional expense for the car repairs and because it was not part of original quote, and not budgeted, he allowed me some time to pay the bill. The work done on the car was impeccable. Under the hood was spotless and some kind of adjustment was needed for the driver's side door which he did at no further cost. The kindness of this man and the kindness of G-d for connecting me with him. So very grateful! Gary also offered to help me find a place to spend the night and told me to call if I needed him to assist me. Another very kind gesture and a bonus considering the rather weary few weeks I had just come through.

December 21, 2016: Leaving Austin For The Last Time

I have been driven to study deeply the need for biological DNA realignment and have discovered the necessity of bringing people out of their pain and suffering. This will be addressed in my future writings.

"Honor your father and your mother this is the first commandment with a promise that it may go well with you and you will live long on the earth." (Ephesians 6:2)

We have never seen such unwarranted abusive things that seniors go through in this pampered generation, who seem to be devoid of understanding the spiritual consequences. I wrote an entire chapter on this in my first book. I took responsibility for what I have long ago repented from and will not be a victim!

My Additional Day In Austin

I had a lot of errands to do in Austin the next day. I was able to get a haircut that I had prepaid for on Groupon, get my phone updated; my iPad looked at and booked an inexpensive hotel in North Austin for the night. Ladybug and I slept well! I purchased some food for the road, and as I came out of the store, there was a homeless man asking for help. I looked at what I had bought and gave some to him. It just crushes me to see so much need.

The next day, we left for Dallas. I had to pick up clothes left too long at a cleaner's, get Ladybug to a groomer and do a few errands that needed to be done. I had a health issue that I should have gone to the doctor for while in Austin, which I foolishly didn't take care of. Definitely not a wise choice! I was in a hurry to get to Dallas and then off to Louisiana for the next ten days.

The Invitation To Louisiana: Emotional Triggers; Unhealed Life Of Pain; Abuse Deeply Connected To Witchcraft

I was eagerly waiting to spend some refreshing and relaxing time in

Louisiana for the Christmas Holidays through an invitation from a single mom with whom I had forged a two-year online relationship. We had discussed at great length the plight of the single parent community and the many issues needing to be addressed. We agreed that connecting physically would help us to consider further ways evaluate this topic so dear to G-d's heart. I was not at all prepared for the situation I walked into.

In consideration to those who celebrate Christmas and not knowing the family's traditions, I did not want to arrive on Christmas Eve or Christmas Day. I didn't want to disrupt any family plans. So, I moved swiftly through all of my errands in Texas—two days in Austin and two more days in Dallas. I drove through the night, taking time to rest along the way and arriving in Louisiana early in the morning of the 23rd of December. I had never been to this state before and had no knowledge of its historical roots.

I was looking forward to a pleasant holiday season but arrived at an uninviting, disheveled, squalid environment. I was shocked, to say the least, and totally unprepared to be in a place that would bring another dimension of a continuum of health issues. There were so many young lives with mental instability, dysfunction, and darkness. But I came with finances, clothes food and gifts. I did not come empty handed.

Apparently, there was mold in the building so most of the furniture had been placed in storage. This made it difficult to cook a proper meal or even eat because there was nothing to cook with or set a normal table. What was more shocking to me was that the young lady told me that she didn't cook at all, a basic life skill. The whole situation was not pleasant and extremely disappointing. She told me she often spent the whole day at the gym when her son went to school. Life skills and dedication of time to her projects to expedite a living seemed to be far from her reality.

There is a clear word that people perish for lack of vision and knowledge. It is a given to write the plan and make it plain like the blueprint from heaven for us to make progress. We can engage G-d's leading in this, and He expects us to do so.

It takes disciplined time management to make the needed progress. I had sent her three clients which would have provided financial resources for her, but I found out later she had not booked any of them. These appointments would have netted her about $300.00. This young lady had some real talent, but she did not mix the practical with the natural.

There were many different possible invitations for various events that she had mentioned but for some reason, she did not engage them, or none were suitable to her for us to attend. This was also disappointing; I would have loved to experience the diversity of the culture of the area. When guests come, it is always in the best interest of the hostess to make the event smashing. This social skill was also not considered and sorely lacking.

On the actual day of Christmas, we went out to a Chinese restaurant which humorously, is always a sure staple to be opened on an American holiday. I'm sure it is a very profitable day for Chinese business owners. I'm laughing at the thought of it. We awaited the young woman's children to join us. It had no normal holiday feeling. The restaurant was crowded, and the service was not good. The children were disrespectful to their mother, desiring, as an activity, lots of photos as we walked along the waterway. Clearly, there were no warm trappings of a family in celebration; very peculiar, but I was a bit exhausted from my weeks of shifting and moving.

The situation did not change for the next few days and was not restful in any way. It was an unhealthy place, and I was saddened to experience it, but it afforded me another opportunity to observe and to understand the fractured lives of the broken in spirit and the broken in heart.

I had inquired about some teachings she was connected to, wanting understanding and application but could not see its relevance in this short time. I had wanted to spend some time with her son, who did not have a relationship with his father, to engage him in a food product that we have developed, but the opportunity never arose, and there were practical things needed to use the kitchen. It seemed this situation would not allow a contribution.

When I departed Louisiana, I drove briefly through New Orleans as I left the state. It is a place most noted for people visiting its French quarter for holidays and vacations. I had never been in the state before, but to me, it was spiritually very dark, dreary with swampy land that went on forever.

I drove down Bourbon Street, but it creeped me out. Perhaps, the familiar spirits in the atmosphere were of whatever kind of depravity it draws year after year for decadent displays of revelry. It was an area known for corruption and the home of the foundation of the secret society known as Free Masons. To me, it reeked of the evil and darkest of this dark foreboding element. I was so glad to leave, and I don't want to ever go back again! All I could think about was the horror of hurricane Katrina as I rushed past the famous convention center, with flashbacks of the news of this horrible encounter. It was as if I could feel it through the peripheral of the New Orleans area on my way out of the state! I still felt the disparity of that event lingering in the atmosphere.

A dear friend of mine had been sent to New Orleans the week before Katrina to pray for repentance in this area for all of the iniquitous deeds done on this land. Clearly, this tragedy loomed in the wake of his prayers as a sent one to this area. I should have never been invited to stay there. The family was not in a place to receive guests. It was alarmingly squalid, dark and unkempt. There was no daily structure or commitment to appointed times.

Why was I encountering the depravity and condition of so many "leaders" who appeared to be so dysfunctional? If called to lead, they have yet to define the demonstration of true and undefiled religion which is at the heart of the sojourner. These debilitating situations needed to be understood and help extended to those whose conditions or needs could only be met in community involvement. There was way too much brokenness and isolation.

I hated being the mistreated sacrificial lamb if you will. But this journey was one that I was commissioned to, and it must be walked out to produce these very writings and the awareness of true hospitality to the temporarily disenfranchised!

My greatest hope and heart's cry is, *"mercy Lord on the human condition that no one sees, nor do they stop along the way to get the game plan and go all the way to the end and complete the circle as the Jewish people do."*

My difficulty in all that I had been exposed to in the last several months was me not discerning properly. I had not sought eternal counsel from the Spirit of Wisdom and the Spirit of Counsel. These are two wonderful aspects of G-d we can engage in from Him to receive clear direction. This was my gravest error. I was caught off guard and found I needed to better understand that until you meet someone in person, a friendship cannot be properly forged or established. In many cases, where there has historically been much domestic violation, abuse, and baggage, to say it was deceptive and alarming is an underestimation.

As the Hebrew language is being revived and studied today, it is considered a pure, three dimensional and pictorial language. Here is a Hebrew letter *"vav."* The modern Hebrew name for the letter waw is *vav,* a word meaning *"peg"* or *"hook."* When used as a consonant, it has a *"v"* sound and as a vowel, it has a *"ow"* and *"uw"* sound. The Hebrew letter states in context *"what the eye hooks into, you become."* I believe this was the state of the mental condition of this family. Too much focus on the dark side and too much background into the occult with huge residual effects.

The darkness and dark side of the fall of Satan is related to that phrase. The most magnificent of creatures fell from hooking his eye into pride and jealousy. Out of pursuing the depths of darkness, it becomes the focus. There is so much glory and power that counters the darkness that is around us. We are to shift our thoughts and meditations from and connecting with darkness once we are delivered into glory, or we will invite it to be part of the fabric of our lives. It's G-d's goodness that brings us to repentance, healing joy, and full restoration. The battles belong to G-d, and He brings us into a place of refreshing in due time.

My heart hurts for the depth of the woundedness of the disenfranchised in each generation. My host in Louisiana was a single mom who had been through some dark times in her life and these experiences had caused her to develop a victim mentality. There is a back story of dark engagement with male dominated, depraved alignment/society, in the family bloodline with emotional and generational abuses. If we have never experienced a father's love and have never been "daddy's girl," we may convince ourselves that we have a keen, spiritual understanding of love, but keep looking for love in all the wrong places. We don't know how to properly build or wait for the G-dly relationship. It is fervently pursued but never attained.

What is sorely lacking is teaching to mentor one as how to look for the one that will provide a wonderful friendship. Necessary training is needed on how to court one another properly, honor each other as the partner we want to be, and show us how to be on the path to prepare for a wonderful covenant marriage. I love the Jewish belief system that states they believe our husbands come from heaven. This is G-d's original plan which He has never deviated from but is so misaligned today.

I had to experience this firsthand to see there are many hurting people in this nation. Hidden secrets, false perceptions and lack of what should have a community involvement, were not evident. We need skilled leaders who can train these broken vessels, and shift the fractured out of these hopeless, fatherless and abusive environments.

There is a need for role models who are educated in life skills who can demonstrate what it is to be in healthy home environments and relationships. Mature and authentic leaders - not ones who have overtones of "religion" yet do not possess a deep understanding of what is necessary to have and build strong relationships.

The Challenges Are Increasing Among Single Parents As Divorce Is Rampant, Or Children Are Born Out Of Wedlock.

There are some (and perhaps very few) faith-based institutions in our society that are being challenged to make these specific areas important factors. Providing assistance and backing to single parent families must be top priority in decision making. A viable plan that clearly shows a way to meet the needs and a community support is sorely needed.

From my trip to Louisiana, I surmised that there has to be a balance of being productive in society to become the best success through life's trials and misses. We must be outside of the four walls in the community becoming the hands of love to those who desperately need what institutional religion has not provided in the past. It was overwhelming for me to see the state of this situation.

Atlanta, Georgia

I left Louisiana about 3:00 p.m. and traveled seven hours straight through to Atlanta with just a few stops. I prayed the entire time while I was driving. Ladybug and I had some good fruit and veggies to eat along the way, and of course, she had her dog food. Night driving for me is not the most fun so as soon as I knew we had entered the Georgia border we stopped for the last time to get gas. It was time that we needed to pull over to rest and to get some sleep.

When I woke up, it was still very, very early. We got back on the road and headed to Atlanta, a place I had not been to for eleven years. I felt the Lord say, *"this is a city of destiny."* The first time I came to Atlanta was in 2000 on a speaking engagement. Because I was involved in the business sector, I had returned several times to teach at various events and also had a few television appearances. I know a lot of people here but from a very different time and season which was more focused on business and the marketplace. It was teaming with movement, with a focus on prayer for the business community. But this time, it was different—a very different time.

The leaders of that time and season had allowed themselves to become obsolete and out of step with the current global conditions and thus, were still stuck in that season. I would find that the people from my former days would not reconnect, and I knew it was because G-d had much different plans for me in this season.

Mid-Town Atlanta

My dear friend Hunter, who was helping me in this transition, had friends and family here. He took it upon himself to book me at the lovely Highland Inn in midtown Atlanta. I loved the feel of the charming mid-century hotel that I stayed in. It had an old-world European charm. It reminded me of my travels throughout Europe. The older part of Atlanta was undergoing gentrification and had its issues with forcing people out of the now expensive real estate. It was very cold when I arrived, and I was about to experience this east coast weather for the first time.

The hotel had a little kitchen with free breakfast, and it was great to have a morning nosh and meet some younger people who were native to the area. One new friend, Gibson, whom I engaged in conversation, had a brilliant mind. He took me to a map on the wall to show me areas of this great city. He took the time to explain its history and the shifts that was happening here like in so many other areas. He had a heart for the underdog and had seen people shifted out of affordable housing, having no place to go. He was a world traveler and had a lot of compassion. We had some stimulating conversations about the historical things I would learn about the city of Atlanta.

Atlanta had an ice storm that week, which I had never experienced before! Not only was it freezing but ice was all over the car and walkways. I was to learn that it is rather dangerous to be out in such a weather! So, I had my first experience slipping and sliding helplessly on icy sidewalks!

It was rather humorous trying to get dog food out of a car that was now frozen shut. Salt had to be poured out on the sidewalks and stairs, so there would be no injuries from slipping. This Californian girl was beginning to understand the southern east coast winter weather! Brrr! I was told that the worst part is that I may have to stay indoors because those icy roads can be very dangerous. So, this little boutique hotel became my warm, cozy location for the entire week. Fortunately, there was a market close by that had a daily soup menu so I could get something warm to eat, so I was set. It must have felt worst for little Ladybug. She did have to go out for a bit of a walk and even clothed in two sweaters she was still shivering!

Mid-town has its charm. What I liked was the old brick Sears and Roebuck building on Ponce Avenue, now called the Ponce Building. It was a historical building now carved up into many stores and restaurants. The top floor boasted the Roof Top with a dance pavilion, a large beer garden, and other outdoor eating places. The building was built in 1929, and I saw lots of old photos of this iconic structure. The company was reminiscent of my childhood because in those days, Sears, as it was later called was a catalog store where everyone ordered everything pertaining to the household. It would have been equal to Amazon today. Even though they are still re-gentrifying a lot of this area, it is rather nice to have some of the old-world charms of a gone by era to enjoy.

Another Open Door: Another Insight

I didn't know where I would go next and thought we would have to spend a night or two in the car. Fortunately, we got a call that prevented us from having to go back to a more vulnerable state!

A very attractive woman, who had a very sweet spirit and an equally beautiful smile provided us with our next residence in an Atlanta suburb. She received Ladybug and me and I was grateful. The place was located north of the hotel I was currently staying next to Alpharetta. It reminded me a lot of Orange County. The last time I was in the Alpharetta area was 2005 on a visit of discovery. I came to Atlanta to see if I would like to move here at that time. Alpharetta had been very much out in the country in those days, but now, it was a much different and booming landscape.

January was a lot colder in Atlanta than where I had been before. There was rain and winds and we had to stay bundled up — getting used to colder weather now.

Like many people, my hostess had hit a rough spot and was in the process of going back to work. It was a great relief for her to be getting back on track after an extended test. She had been stretched but was now among the working class again. When I came, she was having to stand for the miraculous for some of her funds.

Meeting Up With Gibson To View Innovative Ideas

I was hoping to be able to work on Ladybug Loves Products going for some measure of sustainability. Although there is an extended kindness, it is still a challenge because it is someone else's kitchen. There is still a dilemma because things have to be prepared and stored and so much more.

I decided to take my young friend Gibson, whom I met from the Highland Inn Hotel in mid-town to lunch. We met near the beltline area of Atlanta with a huge millennial and Gen Z population. He took me into a fantastic building with an incredible food area considered the new innovative way to do business among the young. Pop-up restaurants of many varieties all individually structured inside one large conventional building with a huge common seating area. It was the weekend, and it was teeming with people enjoying the foods of many businesses. It was an amazing place to visit and to see a newer innovative way of building local companies in such an incredible method.

I gave Gibson some of my Ladybug Loves cake balls to try, and he devoured them. I am not sure if he was just hungry, or they hit the spot with him! His comment was *"dangerously delectable."* This visit gave me a lot of food for thought for building business models on future generations and blending the old and new for an innovative, productive business.

Meanwhile, Back At My Current Living Accommodations

I was so grateful for the provision of a place to stay out of the elements It was now very cold weather. When in someone else's home, it has to be harmonious for the person who is kind to assist and perhaps shift things emotionally and comfortably. Flexibility can become difficult with challenges when things that are not the norm in an emotionally healthy home.

I had immediately suggested that we could begin to pray together frequently, and we did a few times. But to engage in the kind of consistency that would shift both of our lives, would require an aggressive, powerful, worshipping nature to shift the atmosphere and bring in a realm of spiritual openness. This is very difficult to do in another's home. It could have been awesome.

On entrance to this home, there were a lot of packing boxes; plastic container stacked up in all rooms and storage bins on the peripheral of a three-bedroom home, as well as some pieces of furniture. The young lady shared some of her journey with me. She had sustained a back injury and had a lot of out-of-town travels. That explained the clutter I had noticed when I first arrived. But now, I was to find out that she had lived with this in every room, in a 3-bedroom home for three years. This was more than peculiar considering she lived alone with no pets.

Of course, I was grateful for a place to sleep, so I just maneuvered around the bed framed by large plastic bins and layers of clothes hung on doors outside of the closets. I didn't even bring suitcases inside as there was no room to put them. I just brought what I needed and no more.

This young lady had a very formidable passion of being a raw vegan for many years. It was the very fiber of her kitchen rituals and life. There had to be a lot of understanding of how to function in this kind of sanctuary. It was a sacred place.

I finally purchased my own kitchen utensils and placed all foods that were non-perishable out into my car and resorted to eating outside of the kitchen as much as possible. Very occasionally, I would cook the likes of organic chicken. Thank G-d I don't eat beef as it was not allowed in this vegan's kitchen and I do respect that.

Understandably this would be difficult for this kind of lifestyle and though grateful, it was strenuous at best. I didn't want to be a liability. This was to be a very temporary place to stay and it was proving hard to contribute. I was doing all that I could to find out how to become viable. I did attend some interesting start-up ideas for the city, North of Atlanta where I am now staying. But alas, without one's own home, this presented its own perplexing set of circumstances.

I began to feel that very challenging area of becoming *a non-entity* with no identity in the natural world. Without a permanent address, getting my car insured in the state of Georgia would be impossible and I could not use P.O. Box for an address. I was now realizing that without a permanent home one can lose their identity and ability to function properly. Had this not happened to me personally, I would not have understood the myriads of people living with this very challenging loss in one of the most prosperous nations in the world.

In the many places I have had the privilege to stay, the hardest of all is that there is very little understanding of our spiritual identity. I was seeing a huge wave that is nationwide - people existing with no real identity. Some may have a spiritual understanding, and many have a religious spirit but there is a striving for true identity, and it is rampant. We are designed with a desire for producing what our passion is on earth, and clearly it must be to extend ourselves to touch the masses around us in a very significant way.

Our True Identity

"My frame was not hidden from You when I was being formed in secret [and] intricately and curiously wrought [as if embroidered with various colors] in the depths of the earth [a region of darkness and mystery]. Your eyes saw my unformed substance, and in Your book all the days [of my life] were written before ever they took

shape, when as yet there was none of them. How precious and weighty also are Your thoughts to me, O G-d! How vast is the sum of them! If I could count them, they would be more in number than the sand. When I awoke, [could I count to the end] I would still be with You." (Psalm 139:15-18 AMPC)

If G-d opens a door where you have to be at the mercy of people at any time in your life, you know how humbling it can be. Our societal norms have become an ever-shifting movement in the last decade. We have become an unrecognizable culture from just twenty years ago. We have become a trending cultural sacrifice as we classify age groups by a cataloged name such as "baby- boomers," "millennials," etc. Our culture has shifted radically, and it is important to stay flexible in uncomfortable places.

Why is there so much pressure in simple things? We take things that sandpaper us way too seriously. Perspective is so important. It has been an education. In all my years, I have never been without a permanent home for such a long season as this. The lack of appreciation we have for the comfort of one's own residence is mind-boggling at best! The many encounters with people who pass through so many varying situations of being disenfranchised differs. It can be a slippery slope for those without a network of any sort, or a little faith or belief that they will ever rise again. It has not been that case for me, but I did have some very close encounters.

Nevertheless, I have been allowed to experience some of this, to become a voice and to understand the need for community that is warm, caring and authentic. Often this does not exist for those who can reach out or who are to be the hands extended. This should not be. We need to shift from "me" thinking to "we" thinking.

"Whoever is kind to the poor lends to the Lord, and He will reward them for what they have done." (Proverbs 19:17 NIV)

An Elderly Lady, Alone, Scared And 90 Years Old

Today, I read a very sad story of a 90-year-old woman. She was living all alone in fear and despair but had the fortitude, (thank G-d) to walk to her next-door neighbor's home and left a handwritten note on the door that said *"I am 90 years old; I am lonely, alone and afraid. All of my friends have died. Will you be my friend?"*

Gut-wrenching! I read this with a broken heart. I am so happy that she took the initiative to step out. But why don't we innately care and seek our neighbors out? Why have we become so detached, especially to the elderly who need us? Where is true compassion and extending our hands in love? What happened to neighborliness and caring for others in our communities? We are a hardened society. People simply need each other.

The heart of the Father is to protect all people especially those who need compassion and companionship. We need to seek G-od's voice early each day to see how we can share His love to those around us who are in all sorts of pain. We simply need to hear and obey that inner voice.

The Next Lesson And Understanding Of The Human Condition

I would be getting a permanent residence very soon and I was so grateful for the invitation by this woman allowing me to stay in her residence. She had been through some extreme financial and business difficulties herself. She had a bit of rigidity about her space and at this moment she was the extension of kindness to me not spending another night in my car.

The little flaws of communal living will be challenged and tested when we are accustomed to living alone. We can lose what the community provides - warmth, congeniality, love, caring and a sense of belonging to one another. Single people need relationships but alas, sometimes they don't understand that community has a sandpapering effect to take the *"me"* out and join the *"we."* Along the road, community needs to be engaged.

Once again, I was in a home that had all windows covered, preventing any light from coming in. I knew my host preferred it this way so if I opened any window during the day, I knew I had to make sure they were all covered and closed by the end of the day when she returned home.

We need light to be healthy; to become light and to thrive for our health and wellness. Light is what G-d stated in creation, *"let there be light."* We love sunshine, and we feel down casted in dreariness and darkness. I think the only thing we like about dreariness is if we are inside a cozy home with a warm, inviting environment and a crackling fire and some lovely, warm beverage to share with beautiful, engaging conversation.

Our homes should be warm and inviting, flooded with joy and laughter! But alas, this journey has often proved that there is such a disparaging need to shift the culture inside one's home and physical heart, as well as out! It is so very hard to see people so isolated and fearful in their homes, which spoke volumes about their spiritual interior that is creating these feelings. Fear and darkness seem to be running rampant across the lives of people who really don't know a G-d of protection and radiant love.

When my host came home in the evenings, I would greet her warmly. That was usually the extent of our contact. She would retreat to her room and I, wanting to give her the freedom and privacy she needed would close my door as well. I got the message and tried to make myself as scarce as possible. Each morning Ladybug and I left early to go for breakfast at a fast-food place. Then, I would take her for her morning walk at the beautiful, modern Avalon mall. I knew I could not use the sacred raw vegan place, "the kitchen," to prepare morning meals. And I wanted to give her as much space as possible while she was at home.

If I am in the kitchen, I tried to make my passage there brief and retreat quickly, to the point that I had my own plates, utensils, a glass and coffee cup and most of my food (non-perishable) was stored in the car. I did have to get instant coffee because I couldn't leave coffee in the pot to later reheat a second cup, it was not allowed. It just seemed the best thing to do under these circumstances. I couldn't seem to get it right upon my usage there, and even though I cleaned up, I was ridiculed for any remaining specks and cell phone pictures with post-it notes on surfaces, in the refrigerator or the pantry and even photographs were rigidly posted to punctuate my ineptness. This had escalated to the point of intimidation while in the kitchen. So sad; the bondage!

Post-it-note On A Noodle

Two nights ago, I saw post-it notes on one pasta noodle on the white tiled kitchen floor as I walked in. I had tried to cook a meal the night before and exited quickly. It was definitely a statement of displeasure. Under the consistent understanding that this kitchen had to meet a very challenging standard, I had taken the time to make sure all surfaces were clean, no spots, crumbs, etc. as the post-it notes come out often and everywhere if there was one slight, miniscule infraction. The reasoning is, there are possible "bugs," of which I have never seen any in the kitchen during my stay there. But I missed an elusive noodle that fell on the white tile floor the other night. How I managed to do that, knowing what I know, eludes me. It is probably my haste to exit this "sanctuary," trying to ensure that it looks as though it had not been used. But a post-it-note on the fallen noodle?

It is one of the most peculiar situations I have ever experienced on this journey, and there have been many. I picked up the dastardly noodle, put it in the garbage disposal so there would be no "bugs" to devour it and multiply. How can a noodle be so significant to cause such a controversy when there are overwhelming needs all around us? In light of the situation, my expectations were quite reasonable in spite of the difficultly of desperately trying to find sustainability without the means to do so quickly!

So, I decided to affix my own post-it-note right on the middle of the microwave door! After months of these notes about the right use of this kitchen, I responded by making my own post-it-note. This time, it just had to be done! It was so extreme that it left me on edge because I had to express the peculiarity of these frustrations. I understood that the crowded piles all around the exterior of the kitchen into the dining room and living room already had its burdens. There were fears of some sort of lack or a hoarding mentality could not be let go of.

I suggested that I could do things around the house to be of service as I was trying to develop in a challenging situation. The state of the very overgrown and unkempt yard could use some help, so I was trying to propose a forward movement. But this too had its own set of circumstances which was met with opposition. It was really difficult for me because my trying to help was met with frustration about "how" it was done and maybe some sort of control. I just knew to give up and stay out of sight. It was a disheartening experience, and quite unreasonable and overreaching, knowing that I am trying to arrange to be in a position to move on, but most grateful to be of service in this situation.

However, in the scheme of things, the story of the 90-year-old lady and many more uncharted stories are the real issues out there in this crazy world. There may be many needs, even next door to some of you reading this book now. Please reach out.

"Will you lay down your life for My sake says G-d?" (John 13:38)

It is much easier to die than to lay down your life, day in and day out, with the sense of becoming very sensitive to the core of what really matters. We are not made for the bright, shining moments of life, but we have to walk in the light of them in our everyday lives. There was only one bright, shining moment in the life of Jesus, and that was on the Mount of Transfiguration. It was there that He emptied Himself of His glory for the second time, and then came down into the demon-possessed valley.

For thirty-three years, Jesus laid down His life to do the will of His Father. *"By this, we know love, because He laid down His life for us. And we also ought to lay down our lives for the others."* Yet, it is contrary to our human nature to do so. We like our pride; we like what sin is and we don't want correction or growth throughout our lives. And most of all, we like to be in control. It isn't fun to be brought low or to desire humility in a very "me" focused life. One must become disparaged of one's self-worth and just become the epitome of what Jesus would do. If I am a friend of Jesus, I must deliberately and carefully lay down my life for Him. It is a difficult thing to do and thank G-d that it is because there is so much of me in me. This is the only way we can become love.

What Does Love Have To Do With It? This is What The World Needs Now

The way of love is written here from the Bible; this following passage needs to be broken down to really get all of the details from it. Everyone is looking for love, to be loved, or to engage in loving relationships. We have to become love! It is essential for us to function daily. Do you feel loved and valued? If you do, then you are so very fortunate.

As I wrote in my first book, affirmation, Fathers love, and intimacy are so foundational to a healthy society, but many suffer from this major lack in their lives. Let's shift this together. Let's gather for a greater good and become an unending community of love in whatever way we can.

"If I speak in the tongues of men and of angels, but have not love, I am a noisy gong or a clanging cymbal. And if I have prophetic powers, and understand all mysteries and all knowledge, and if I have all faith, so as to remove mountains, but have not love, I am nothing. If I give away all I have, and if I deliver up my body to be burned, but have not love, I gain nothing. Love is patient and kind; love does not envy or boast; it is not arrogant or rude. It does not insist on its own way; it is not irritable or resentful; it does not rejoice at wrongdoing but rejoices with the truth. Love bears all things, believes all things, hopes all things, and endures all things. Love never ends. As for prophecies, they will pass away; as for tongues, they will cease; as for knowledge, it will pass away. For we know in part and we prophesy in part, but when the perfect comes, the partial will pass away. When I was a child, I spoke like a child, I thought like a child, I reasoned like a child. When I became a man, I gave up childish ways. For now, we see in a mirror dimly, but then

"face to face. Now I know in part; then I shall know fully, even as I have been fully known. So now faith, hope, and love abide, these three; but the greatest of these is love." (1 Corinthians 13 ESV)

A World Devoid Of Joy: People Need To Be Loved

This was the consensus of my travels; having a form of G-dliness but no power because of the frail human condition and the isolation of people just trying to survive their own trauma with no real community, companionship or joy on the journey.

Relationships should help develop, resolve and sandpaper the issues of the heart. What is sorely needed is an understanding of the way the Jewish mindset teaches to be caring and to embrace everyone no matter what, not religious practices. People need to be heard and honored and developed to bring out their creative forces, to add to and not take away, what is before them.

How does G-d perceive the people who have no real heart of introspection? Why was I engaged to meet these people on the journey? To become love and to learn to love. Every painful encounter caused me to feel the pain of so many who have no hope and who have no community, no real caring friends who understand how to take *just the one* all the way through to victory! Just one!

Graham Cooke's 400-People Challenge

I believe what Graham Cooke, a well-seasoned teacher of unorthodox Christian beliefs, did with a group of people was engaging love. He invited 400 people to take in one homeless person (the same one) into their home once a week. Give them a shower, clean clothes, a meal and a bed; engage them in conversation and work with them just once a week. What a concept of helping the human condition! I am not sure of the timeframe, but I think it lasted a year. I am sorry to say I don't know the final outcome, but knowing how Graham Cooke operates, it must have been a glorious improvement!

In every major city or area in the USA, there is a Jewish community center. I have discovered this along the way. Every age group with pertinent needs is helped by addressing the human condition whether Jewish or not. They know that they are commissioned to take care of the people who come across their path every day. This is why they were born on this earth. You can read it everywhere you turn, on how the prolific Jewish culture is known to be the amazing extension of Abba's love! It is in the unique privilege to be one called "chosen".

I had gotten food at the Jewish community center when I had no food. While on this sojourner journey, I have had my rent paid by them without any questions. They simply asked, *"What else do you need?"* The giving is profuse, and they are blessed! They are raised with the understanding that they live to give! G-d chose a people group which He would miraculously raise up to touch the world! It is uncanny how profoundly they have done what they have done!

My personal goal now is to understand the power of the love so needed in today's chaos. I have so much more to say of the many miracles that I have had in the last year of trying to stabilize my life as He has directed. But this may be all that can be added to this book about the sojourners' journey.

Atlanta, Georgia For One Year

Miraculously I settled in the city of Avondale Estates, Georgia for one year, starting May 17, 2017. It is a sleepy bedroom community of just under 3000 in an Atlanta suburb southeast next to Decatur and not far from where I was living in mid-town Atlanta.

This was another supernatural door that had been opened for me to live, as I could not have gotten into this condo without the help of two amazing women of prayer. One of the ladies had prayed for me when I first came to Georgia to teach almost twenty years ago. The other lady lived next door to the condo that I lived in for nine months. She is well respected in her stream of influence and has a brilliant work to help people in a specialized way. They were sent to me in this season by G-d to get me into a place of my own for this next level of rest and safety.

Everything on this journey is miraculous, and only G-d could have touched hearts to do the unusual. The young man who owed the condo was soon to be married and was rarely in the condo. He only requested two months' rent with a very inexpensive house payment and reduced that by $350.00. Ladybug was bonused in because she was so tiny, and she captivated his heart. The place was literally a man cave and it took me one month to give it my feminine touch. I knew he wanted to sell the condo and I made some very creative offers, but he just wanted it gone. I relished having my own home for nine months. It felt so good to be settled in an environment where I could be me with my own house rules. It felt so good to be settled in an environment where I could be me with my own house rules.

I had hoped to purchase the condo. My dear friend Bill, who had a real estate background, was going to help me but unfortunately at the time he was fighting cancer. Bill was a real treasure; he went to Heaven too soon. The time spent here has been lovely; a gorgeous place to live and I have met wonderful people. I have been very blessed with lovely neighbors here.

The hard fact for Georgia is that the cost of housing is the same here as it is all over our country but not as devastating as other areas like California. The fact is that in 2017, the housing costs, both sales and rentals in Georgia have risen by 11%. The city of Avondale Estates wanted to increase the property taxes by more than 8% in 2018 at the time of this writing. People need to prayerfully understand that affordable housing for sustainability is a necessity for all people everywhere. Purchasing land and building affordable housing is going to be a necessity. We need our own land.

Avondale Estates Georgia

There is a beautiful lake here in the city of Avondale Estates, where I walked Ladybug most of last year and her cuteness has always attracted conversation and many encounters of meeting the friendly residence here on these walks.

One day, I had one very unusual experience while walking Ladybug by the lake. A young lady was standing at the edge of the lake as we were walking by and we could hear her audibly praying very intensely and weeping as she prayed. She faced the lake totally engaged in audible prayer. I paused on the path to listen to her cries. She was lost in her expression and moving devotion, pleading with G-d. Her mother also was praying a little farther down the lake, as I found out later. This young woman is a single parent, and her children were with her mother. She came to the lake to pray "beside the still waters" decreeing the 23rd Psalm as she declared it out loud. She clearly was in earnest and did not care who heard her appeals. I stood on the path for a minute then saw a bench near her and sat behind her and extended my hand toward her, praying in agreement quietly.

At the appointed time, I came up to her and began to encourage her. I put my arms around her, and she sobbed and sobbed and sobbed.

I was able to speak life into her circumstances; shared some of the many miracles that have happened in my life. I continue to pray for her often. Stopping for the one along the way in an extraordinary encounter, just being on the path that day at the lake. I had no set time that I would take Ladybug there to walk, so it was an appointment orchestrated by G-d.

Today, one-third of American children live in a single parent home—a total of 15 million—are being raised without a father. Nearly five million more children live without a mother. Vincent Di Caro, vice president of the National Fatherhood Initiative, blames this trend for many of society's ills. He claims the way to deal with poverty, drugs, crime, and other hot-button cultural issues are to strengthen the two-parent family; deal with absent fathers, he says, and the rest follows. A growing number of studies show that fatherlessness has a major negative impact on the social and emotional development of children.

The young people on the journey are many, and the internal scars are on those who desperately need to change their minds. I've met some of the young leaders in this area who needed guidance; they are hungry. I have been able to reach out to them many times on my walks with Ladybug. I've seen the less motivated older people too, who are stuck and settled, not interested in change. But alas, G-d is doing so much as the storms rage worldwide and we are being formed into another being. This scripture comes to mind to be embraced now.

"For the rest, brethren, whatever is true, whatever is worthy of reverence and is honorable and seemly, whatever is just, whatever is pure, whatever is lovely and lovable, whatever is kind and winsome and gracious, if there is any virtue and excellence, if there is anything worthy of praise, think on and weigh and take account of these things [fix your minds on them]." (Philippians 4:8 AMPC)

To be vulnerable, we have to lay our lives down on a daily basis. It's not a onetime thing, and then we become perfect. Out of pain and suffering, we are to become sensitive to the needs of others. We have to allow inconvenience to shift us out of complacency! There is a new world view that needs to be embraced, and the reality of the human condition cries out for us to be the hand extended to a very chaotic and troubled world.

Home Is Where The Heart Is

The origin of this proverb is unclear, however, the first written instances of *"home is where the heart is"* appeared in the mid-nineteenth century. Perhaps, the earliest of all is in a work by Joseph Neal in 1847. Some people believe that the phrase was said earlier, in the mid-seventeenth century, by the jurist Edmund Coke. It has also been used (later) by famous authors like Robert Burns and Anthony Burgess. Nowadays, people often use it without being aware of the origin.

The Meaning Of This Saying

"Home is where the heart is" can be interpreted in two different ways. As each of these interpretations is in common use, it is worthwhile looking at them both. Firstly, it can mean that *"wherever our loved ones are, that is our home,"* indicating that wherever a person's heart is will be our true home. The real home is the place that they care about most in the world. This may or not be the place where they were born or where they grew up.

Secondly, it can mean that *"our love (our 'heart) is focused on the family home."* It means *"no matter where we are, we will always feel deep love and affection for our home."* A person's heart will always be at home meaning that that their love, affection and fond memories will always be tied to the place that they lived and were brought up. But in today's societies, we have such an increase in the lack of a place to call home and the deficiency of this most basic need causes much devastation.

Wow, this week I was smacked with a thread of revelation on this statement, *"HOME IS WHERE THE HEART IS,"* when I was faced with an all too familiar situation. People with generous hearts who opened their homes to give me a place to stay for a short time. I have had to continue on this road less traveled to learn another facet of a mystery of the Father's heart. This experience taught me that I had walked in presumption and not consulted G-d. I was willing to not look at circumstances but to trust that I would be led by Him even in the most unusual way yet.

When He told me that I would be seeing things through a different lens, He was not kidding. He is clearly showing me that we have to be willing to be willing and really hear *His Heart* in the matter. In everything, there is a lesson and this time, it becomes very, very clear that there are a lot of people's households where chaos is ruling. Chaos, what is it? Here is the description of chaos: disorder, disarray, disorganization, confusion, mayhem, bedlam, pandemonium, havoc, turmoil, tumult, commotion, disruption, upheaval, uproar.

We all have different mindsets, upbringing, and home lives. But in the home, it should be the place to shut out the daily frustrations and come away into an atmosphere of comfort, safety and cleanliness. It should also reflect a place to cocoon with other family members in an emotionally healthy environment. We need to be able to go home and be refreshed, let our hair down, so to speak and rest from the toils and business of the outside world.

Home is a place that should bring warmth, and we should look forward to going home. As individuals, we need to find a routine of making it a functional place of order — divine order. It should take on a personality of the character of who we are and what we represent. There should be fragrances, smells, laughter, atmospheres to create positivity in a warm open environment where peace and tranquility abide—a place of true freedom and safety.

What Is Missing In The Home?

Is it the fragmentation of society over the last fifty years? Are people so negligent that they have forgotten to enjoy and live in a place that is not a house but a home? The evidence is in the places I have visited or stayed for short terms. The alarm has taken me over.

Is it the lack of skilled mothers in the home to peacefully nurture and train the next generation? It's the image of a strong father figure who leads his family by loving their mother, providing for the family financially with protection, wisdom, and provision.

The brokenness and emotional trials usually are as a result of so many absentee fathers today. I've seen some who may be present in the home but don't have positive fathering skills and are passive, aggressively bullying their kids into frustration. They don't train but try to control their children, and they are not spiritual heads of households.

There are some with a current moniker called *"baby daddy"* which resulted in single-parent households crying out from the devastation it has brought on. It seemed as if this way of life has been accepted as our reality. It's the dismissal of the institution of marriage as if it is not a necessity at all. It's the alarming "sexual revolution" that started decades ago and degraded the preciousness of the foundation of culture, the marriage covenant. This is a lost term, but it used to be called Holy Matrimony, and this framework had a true understanding that entering into marriage was not to be taken lightly but a true lifetime commitment and engagement in a relationship with G-d at the helm.

Let's look at the word "covenant." It means contract, agreement, undertaking, commitment, guarantee, warrant, pledge, promise, bond, indenture. We have lost or never been taught to prepare properly for a life's companion because of this. It has been a reckless to engagement in relationships without proper preparation, education, personal esteem, and self-control. There are many, many things that roll around in my mind for the next generation coming up.

The process to change is to bring the right education forward now for a culture in crises. Permissive, casual sex is a devastation and produces a host of ailments in every part of one's life which deeply weakens culture. Attaining a deep, divine connection, ordained companionship that remains pure allows one to intimately, passionately and spiritually enter into union and become one.

Further, in marriage, one of the greatest gifts is virginity, which is grossly mocked today. But we can stop the madness to redeem lost virginity and time through healthy training and recover what has been lost or stolen by the debauched societal issues at hand. We can rise up and shift the generations coming up. Let's desire to heal the most valuable of decisions a life, and I mean *life partner preparation,* that by design, can strengthen and restore our cultural foundations. This is so foreign and lost today. We need a revival of the power of all of this with the strength for a restoration for what has been lost.

A Different Insight

I met a business associate recently who is from the Philippines and we had a great conversation on the process of choosing a marriage partner. According to his culture, they look more circumspectly because they are marrying for life; divorce is not allowed. There can be marital separation if there is abuse or harm, but they cannot remarry. As he expressively stated, *"he married the one he loved and loves the one he married"*. If we had a deep understanding like the Jews do, that your companion comes from heaven, we would not marry quickly, but we would pursue the course of marriage with understanding before we prepare for a wedding celebration.

We need great mentors now in the current generation to restore a great path for progress to loving marriages partnerships. These mentors can be those who has weathered many storms to stay growing in the midst of these external storms thus maturing along life's path. The path of marriage is not to be self-serving but to blend, grow, communicate and to become one.

The Current Affordable Housing Rental Crises

Forty years ago, real estate was conceivably affordable and rental costs was very much the same. Renting a two-bedroom apartment at $300.00 was considered expensive.

I was a single parent from the get-go, as I left my dysfunctional marriage while pregnant with my daughter. But keeping a clean, functional home was a normal thought and fixing a dinner meal for us both while my daughter was young was also normal. This was up until her teenage years when I owned my own business. It was also a normal everyday occurrence. My home was a place of peace, joy, warmth and rest; a place to enjoy away from the clamber of the day. The dinner table should be a place to come together where we sort out and share our events of the day. It should be a place of freedom and laughter.

The Human Heart And Its Importance In The Dictated Direction Of Our Lives

As I studied the teaching from Ian Clayton on the human heart, it began to weave a message that needs to be understood universally. The biggest problem is a lack of understanding or education on the framework of the human heart. We don't understand the contents or components of the heart or the center of our human heart and what the heart is made from. G-d wants to change it (the human heart) and bring something new into it.

The human heart is quite interesting. The first part of our physical body to be formed, it is made up of the exact record of the memory of autosomes and chromosomes from your parents. There are twenty-three chromosomes from the male and twenty-three from the female that come together to procreate. The cells begin to divide and replicate in exact copies of one another. After about ten or fifteen multiplications, there is a little ball of cells. The original cell, where the seed of your father and mother came together in the womb, became enclosed and went into the center of that little conglomeration of cells! Out of that cell the human heart is formed. Your body is formed out of the memory record of what that single cell has inside of it There is a supernatural "flash of light" and the heavenly spirit now becomes a human soul called to earth out of Heaven.

To reiterate, our human body houses our soul (mind, will, and emotions), as well as what has already existed in the DNA of our parents. Included in our DNA are all the previous generations going all the way back to the time of creation of the first Adam. So, in our human form, our "spirit being" is now buried inside a physical human body which becomes a male or a female? So, this is a description of what happens in procreation. Our heart is created!

"My frame was not hidden from You when I was being formed in secret [and] intricately and curiously wrought [as if embroidered with various colors] in the depths of the earth [a region of darkness and mystery]. Your eyes saw my unformed substance, and in Your book all the days [of my life] were written before ever they took shape, when as yet there was none of them. How precious and weighty also are Your thoughts to me, O G-d! How vast is the sum of them! If I could count them, they would be more in number than the sand. When I awoke, [could I count to the end] I would still be with You." (Psalm 139:15-18 AMPC)

Here's what G-d comes to do. He comes to change who you are! The Bible says this: *"G-d puts eternity in our hearts."* What G-d has done is to lead us in the first step to become who we are in His kingdom realm, which gets ignited back into our heavenly identity! We need to meditate on this a bit. And again, our heart receives a window into the realm of eternity, and our heart becomes the doorway. Jesus said, *"I am the door; no man can come unto the Father unless he comes through me."*

Today, it is being widely studied on how we can recreate our DNA and remove issues through our thoughts so that the power we have been given can be released to change times and seasons through rich time. Rich time is the ability to enter into the time frame of iniquitous strongholds of darkness. By entering into this through deep understanding, we are spiritually and supernaturally shifting the culture of our biological DNA.

Through spiritually working out the triggers on our autosomes, which are known to be gray areas, that which needs to be recreated in our DNA will respond to the shift of positivity and total restoration will ensue. This is what your heart is made up of—a different doctoral informational pattern—and it then needs to be released into the proper

DNA structure from the realms of Heaven!

That is why the Bible says, G-d is going to come and take away our stony heart and give us a heart of flesh. It's not about taking out this heart! It is about changing the word, "take away," which doesn't mean to be removed. It means to change or to make it into something totally different. So, we have been taught incorrectly before. Now, G-d is depositing into our spirits, a desire to seek His mysteries in a whole new manner! This is the current place He is taking us to; the revelations of deeper understandings, much like the early believers who followed Him.

Here are some powerful expressions in the scripture that will give us all a perspective if we deeply and clearly meditate on each of them. We see that apart from the cleansing from the daily contaminations of the world's pollution, the heart cannot function to its optimum.

"Create in me a clean heart, O G-d; and renew a right spirit within me." (Psalm 51:10 King James version KJV)

"The heart is deceitful above all things, and it is exceedingly perverse and corrupt and severely, mortally sick! Who can know it [perceive, understand, be acquainted with his own heart and mind]?" (Jeremiah 17:9 AMPC)

"The good man from his inner good treasure brings forth good things, and the evil man out of his inner evil storehouse flings forth evil things." (Matthew 12:35 AMPC)

"Take delight in the Lord and He will give you the desires of your heart." (Proverbs 37:4)

"May these words of my mouth and the meditations of my heart be pleasing in your sight Lord, my rock and my redeemer?" (Psalm 19:14)

"Blessed are the pure in heart for they shall see G-d." (Matthew 5:9)

"Keep and guard your heart with all vigilance and above all that you guard, for out of it flow the issues of life." (Proverbs 4:23 AMPC)

We need to understand that without effort, we should be getting the protocols directly out of Heaven! Once we tap into eternity and become love, we flow in dimensions of a different realm and nature. Our sole desire is to produce this in those around us. As we release the sound of the spirit, which is a primordial call, spirit to spirit, we are breaking apart the command centers of darkness over our portion, our territory or assignment, thus becoming the voice for those who need representation.

People are awaiting your obedience to fulfill their destinies and realign with their election and G-d's original plan for them. But perhaps, your understanding will not be as casual as it has been. We have a formidable agenda on our own personal DNA seed line and an assignment to be the embodiment of G-d's love and original plan in what we must understand today. His mysteries are being revealed so that we can do something on earth in an expression which was written on our personal scrolls, for we are called to touch those around us in the streams of influence that we govern.

There are many ways to bring revitalization to the masses. Jesus had only twelve, and today, they are still historically known worldwide for over 2000 years and their teachings are still shifting cultures. We should have the desire and the ability to bring people groups together to take people out of this downtrodden turn. We must find a way to bring this debacle to a close. So, what can you do now? Start with just one. There is a G-d given inspiration inside of each individual to be the solution to the problems or the needs.

In conclusion, we are all on a unique journey to be a voice according to our assignments in this season on earth. There is a crescendo on the horizon of the restoration of all things. But much is being dismantled, and everyone who is reading this can relate in their private journey, that it simply isn't life or business as usual.

Shifting The Agenda In Nations

There are some young voices that are coming out of hiding, who have not liked what they perceive and are becoming the voice of reason. They are utilizing social media platforms, and their video blogs are getting recognition. They are diverse, bold and powerful, speaking to the dying breed of old physical and political agendas that do not spell out their foundational beliefs. What should have been the ceiling for the older leaders has become the foundation for the next generation of fresh authentic and clean new voices.

The harsh reality reminds me of the green witch in the Wizard of Oz as she melted into the floor and stated, *"I'm melting, I'm melting,"* and withered completely into a pile on the floor with no ability to dominate again. Like today, the old decayed agenda and plan are now irrelevant. These young leaders are grabbing the attention in media both in strength and weakness. They are the sent ones to this season in time, to assist in shifting the culture back to reason and success.

There are those who are building on the platform of their natural gifting, and they cannot be shouted down by the generation who is tottering on being aged out because they have made themselves redundant, abide in cronyism and have corrupted our national integrity. They need to bow out of the world's stage and disappear from their dead platforms! It is clearly a new day of arising into the things that will restore humanity. The missing link is deep, moral values and the original plan of a country or nation *under* G-d.

There are those who have been on a spiritual journey and have entered behind the veil, coming out of the normal "religious" encounters, out of the institutions and have become part of the power that can shift a culture by engaging G-d in new ways; ways of real power and a love that restores all things.

There are more power, more compassion and more delegated young leaders who are beginning to storm the gates of hell and iniquity nationally, politically and spiritually. It is a delightful sound to be part of the shift and become the hand behind the generations coming up, who are so significant and so needed today. There is hope and power awaiting us as we support them and their directive. I, for one, have many stirring plans to work in this arena.

When I was introduced to the ensuing shift almost twenty years ago by my mentor, she spoke *that there is a sound of the spirit.* It is a primordial cry, spirit to spirit, and it is written that that all creation is groaning for the manifestation of the sons of God. She was given the visual to see the people in nations who had no rudder, and she has traveled the world doing amazing things.

So, we stand today at the gateway to see the things that are being prepared. And we are moving into dimensions and eternal understanding of the greatness to be used now in this amazing time on earth.

And now, one last penned post and a provisional assignment.

August 28, 2018

Oakland, San Francisco August 27, 2018—The most expensive city in the nation and the increased homeless population is obvious.

Today, I went to San Francisco on Bart to get a copy of my birth certificate. I can't believe that I went into San Francisco from the East Bay and had the opportunity to be here to do it. I got a few copies so that I can now get a Georgia Driver's License. My order never came through from the internet! Ugh!

I went to the Fruitvale Bart station to take the fastest and most economical route to get there. A lot had changed since I was last here in 2012 and I had to ask for help for how to pay. The tickets that you use to pop in and pop out were replaced with a plastic card with a tap to access like a fob at the entrance and exit stalls. The parking was complicated also, no kiosks. You take your parking space number and pay with cash only that is logged into a "book." I came back from my trip to find a $55.00 parking ticket because the parking cop did not "check" the logbook! This is certainly not a good system for a "tourist," but I was able to get up to the train platform to get on the train.

I noticed that the median age ridership was probably mid-30s, an interesting observation with a little mixture. I managed to get to the Civic Center exit and had three flights of stairs to climb out of the underground trains. Surely, with the elderly and infirmed, they must have an escalator, but I did not see one.

I got to the majestic building and was in awe of its antiquity and grandness, something I never admired while living and driving in and out of San Francisco years ago. It's interesting what we can discover when we thoughtfully take the time to stop and observe. I took some pictures inside of the grand stately staircase of an era gone by, all part of a whole other generation. This building looked right out of an old movie from the '40s. Even the elevator was grand with wood paneling which was beautifully detailed. On the sign above the elevator was the word "car" as it was called bygone days.

I stopped at the Powel Street exit on my way back to get a light snack on my return to the East Bay at the Nordstrom's Center. I walked up to Union Square to sit and ponder on a city that I may not see again very soon. I pondered many times—in many decades that I had been there for many different reasons and seasons—how San Francisco has changed and now it is the most expensive city to live in our nation.

I struck up a conversation with a lovely French girl who had just arrived and had visited the city twelve years earlier with her family. She was travelling alone, and I tried to give her some wisdom that this "romantic" city was not as nice as twelve years prior. We had a lovely conversation. What was epic is that she noticed the extreme homelessness in San Francisco, and it was quite prevalent! There were so many people in various sorts of dysfunction and need along the well-traveled tourist foot traffic up and down Powell Street. It was deplorable as the masses move around it and it grieved me terribly. The travesty hurts my heart deeply, and I mourned what is obvious. I was a bit fatigued and could not bear to record it with pictures on my return to continue back on Bart.

I got back to my hotel in the East Bay and had my drapes open with a view of the 880 freeway and the fading sun as the evening lights popped on along the not-too-distant walk, which was just across the freeway divider. I watched from my warm, comfortable hotel room, yet another homeless person with a bright orange vest normally worn by city workers. This one was pushing a grocery cart full of belongings along the street, and again, the despair of such a one, touched me deeply. Our tragic increase of exploding homelessness now in a city that is totally unaffordable for the most vulnerable, the lower *"middle"* class that is no more, the poor living right before our eyes in a ruthless, wealthy city of imbalances. What are we doing about it? Are you ready to help?

I have peppered the book with some meditative scriptures as we need a real roadmap. I leave you here with some very wise thoughts for those who will be compelled to go deep into this need and to know one human being alone cannot change all of this; it will take all of us. These are here and there to provoke a deeper level of needed wisdom in the world that is shifting all around us.

Let us come deeply into rest as our Abba tenderly shifts us to His greater glory from Heaven to earth!

Exaltation Of The Afflicted Isaiah 61 (AMPC)

"The Spirit of the Lord G-d is upon me, because the Lord has anointed and qualified me to preach the Gospel of good tidings to the meek, the poor, and afflicted; He has sent me to bind up and heal the broken hearted, to proclaim liberty to the [physical and spiritual] captives and the opening of the prison and of the eyes to those who are bound, to proclaim the acceptable year of the Lord [the year of His favor] and the day of vengeance of our G-d, to comfort all who mourn, to grant [consolation and joy] to those who mourn in Zion—to give them an ornament (a garland or diadem) of beauty instead of ashes, the oil of joy instead of mourning, the garment [expressive] of praise instead of a heavy, burdened, and failing spirit—that they may be called oaks of righteousness [lofty, strong, and magnificent, distinguished for uprightness, justice, and right standing with G-d], the planting of the Lord, that He may be glorified .And they shall rebuild the ancient ruins; they shall raise up the former desolations and renew the ruined cities, the devastations of many generations .Aliens shall stand [ready] and feed your flocks, and foreigners shall be your plowmen and your vinedressers. But you shall be called the priests of the Lord; people will speak of you as the ministers of our G-d. You shall eat the wealth of the nations, and the glory [once that of your captors] shall be yours. Instead of your [former] shame you shall have a twofold recompense; instead of dishonor and reproach [your people] shall rejoice in their portion. Therefore, in their land they shall possess double [what they had forfeited]; everlasting joy shall be theirs. For I the Lord love justice; I hate robbery and wrong with violence or a burnt offering. And I will faithfully give them their recompense in truth, and I will make an everlasting covenant or league with them. And their offspring shall be known among the nations and their descendants among the peoples. All who see them [in their prosperity] will recognize and acknowledge that they are the people whom the Lord

has blessed. I will greatly rejoice in the Lord, my soul will exult in my G-d; for He has clothed me with the garments of salvation, He has covered me with the robe of righteousness, as a bridegroom decks himself with a garland, and as a bride adorns herself with her jewels. For as [surely as] the earth brings forth its shoots, and as a garden causes what is sown in it to spring forth, so [surely] the Lord G-d will cause rightness and justice and praise to spring forth before all the nations [through the self-fulfilling power of His Word]."

Let me leave you with this famous meditation, often declared, by St. Francis of Assisi.

Prayer Of Peace From Saint Francis Of Assisi

"Lord, make me an instrument of your peace:
Where there is hatred, let me sow love.
Where there is injury, pardon.
Where there is doubt, faith.
Where there is despair, hope.
Where there is darkness, light.
Where there is sadness, joy.
O divine Master, grant that I may not so much seek
To be consoled as to console,
To be understood as to understand,
To be loved as to love.
For it is in giving that we receive,
It is in pardoning that we are pardoned,
And it is in dying that we are born to eternal life."

Bibliography

The Amplified Bible (Classic Version) -
Scriptures are taken from the Amplified Bible (Classic Version), Old Testament copyright 1965 by the Zondervan Corporation. The Amplified New Testament Copyright 1958, 1957 by Lochmann Foundation. Used by permission in the United States of America.

Kintsugi - The Art of Precious Scars, Living by author Stefano Carnazzi, (Translated from Italian) taken off of the enclosed article from the internet.

Sojourner from the Jewish perspective via internet research.

Bernard Madoff obtained via internet research.

Enron Crises taken from internet, researching Housing crises and statistics of the lack of affordable housing, i.e. California and Texas by research taken off of the internet.

Published story on *Svend Petersen*, comments taken from YouTube channel.

Comments taken from the back of the book by *Jason C.N. Jordan* - Lightning from the Master's House

Quote from *Christina Shay's* Facebook account.

Prayer of *St. Francis of Assisi* taken from the internet through research.

Various Quotes from *Ian Clayton* page 143

About The Author

Ann Bandini is an established author/writer. Her most sought-after book is *Second Edition Prayer Strategy: God's Provocative Plan for Wealth.*

In her current release, she addresses what has been brewing across the USA and the nations for much of the five years that she has been prepared for what is a national and international crisis, the lack of affordable housing, increased homelessness and measurable loss of the middle class. She also addresses the disparity of the bulging explosion of epic proportions all over our nation and many western nations to an unconscionable rate.

Ann has had first-hand observation of the issues affecting the moral spiritual and social virtue of the nations and the coming generations as she was commissioned in 2015 to "become a sojourner for a season." This took her through five states in three years. She was to experience, observe and chronicle what she was given to see, experience, discover and narrate. She stepped out of her comfort and security and has come forward from a different perspective.

Ann has owned her own business and worked independently in the beauty industry, constantly reinventing herself to stay with current trends. She was well established in Southern Californian for 30 years.

Her life experiences have equipped her as one full of wisdom, counsel and strong leadership abilities with a mentoring background. Currently, she is addressing and becoming a voice to restore people to their former position by building the proper multidimensional foundations.

Ann's heart is to stop for the one, find out people's passion, and become love! What are we going to do about it?

www.ingramcontent.com/pod-product-compliance
Lightning Source LLC
Chambersburg PA
CBHW060049100426
42742CB00014B/2757